YES, THERE IS A GOD

And Other Answers to Life's Big Questions

D0192528

YES, THERE IS A GOD

And Other Answers to Life's Big Questions

JOHN BERGSMA

the WORD among us® Press

Copyright © 2017 by John Bergsma

All rights reserved

Published by The Word Among Us Press
7115 Guilford Drive, Suite 100
Frederick, Maryland 21704
www.wau.org

21 20 19 18 17   1 2 3 4 5

ISBN: 978-1-59325-310-3
eISBN: 978-1-59325-494-0

Unless otherwise noted, Scripture texts used in this work are
taken from The Catholic Edition of Revised Standard Version
Bible, copyright © 1965, 1966 by the Division of Christian
Education of the National Council of the Churches of Christ
in the United States of America. Used with permission. All
rights reserved.

Cover design by Faceout Studios
Illustrations rendered by Jacob Popcak

No part of this publication may be reproduced, stored in
a retrieval system, or transmitted in any form or by any
means—electronic, mechanical, photocopy, recording, or any
other—except for brief quotations in printed reviews, without
the prior permission of the author and publisher.

Made and printed in the United States of America

Library of Congress Control Number: 2017941008

Table of Contents

Chapter 1

Hello!

Hi there!

Allow me to introduce myself. My name is John.

I was born in Hawaii. I live in Ohio. *The Empire Strikes Back* is one of my favorite movies, and barbecued spareribs is my favorite food.

Okay, enough small talk. I'd like to talk to you about the Big Questions, the things people usually talk about only late at night with friends after a party or on long road trips.

Sometimes these questions are called GLUE: God, Life, the Universe, and Everything.

This is me. →

(I have glasses. When I'm not wearing my contacts.)

And this is you. →

(I hope this is what
you look like.)

And we are together on this planet, hurtling through
space. →

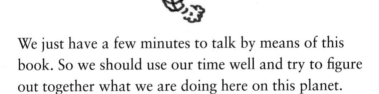

We just have a few minutes to talk by means of this
book. So we should use our time well and try to figure
out together what we are doing here on this planet.

Why are we here?

Did someone put us here?

Is there a purpose for our being here?

If so, what are we supposed to be doing?

These are some of the GLUE questions.

It seems like most of these GLUE questions come down to this:
Is there a Someone who put us here, or not?

If there is a Someone who put us here,
then there probably is a purpose for us to be here
and something we are supposed to be doing.

If there is no Someone who put us here,
then probably everything is an accident
and there is nothing in particular that we should be doing.

Now, usually people have called the Someone "God."

"God" is different from "gods." When we talk about gods, we just mean supernatural beings.

But God with a "capital G" is the Creator, a Being who made everything but was not himself made by anything.

Some ask, "Who made God?" but that's a misunderstanding of what *God* means.

God is eternal. No one made him, because he has always existed. He made everything else. That's what it means to be God.

We want to ask: is there such a Being? A great Someone?

I'll tell you right from the start: I hope there is Someone out there.

If there is, it means there might be hope for us.

Hope that there's a reason we're here.

Hope for a future after we die or this rock we call earth hits something.

Hope that there's something Good at the end of this story we're in.

On the other hand, if there is no one out there and we're here by accident, it seems a little depressing. That means there's no reason or purpose to all of this.

We just wait in the lonely universe until we die or the rock hits something.

If we find out that's just the way it is, I guess I'll deal with it. But I hope Someone is out there.

Still, hoping something is true doesn't make it true. We have to ask the Big Questions and see if there is some evidence for an answer.

So this is the first Big Question I'd like to talk with you about:

Is there a God?

Chapter 2

Is There a God?

So is there a Someone out there who put us here and has a plan for us?

If so, there is probably a purpose for why we are here. And something we should be doing.

If not, then we are probably here by accident, and we don't need to do anything in particular.

Now, maybe you already believe in God. Many people have a strong sense that God exists and don't need an argument or a proof. One person I know of came to believe in God just from looking at a beautiful tree in the fall. Another began to believe when he looked at his baby daughter's ear one day and saw how lovely it was.

If you're the type of person who just knows in your heart there is a God, you might want to skip to the next chapter.

However, if you are the more skeptical type and would like a reason to believe something, then this chapter is for you.

I'd like to offer you some reasons to believe in God. These reasons come from looking around us as we hurtle along on this rock we call the earth.

Looking Up

First, let's look up at the stars, planets, and galaxies above us.

When we do this, we notice something strange. All the stars and galaxies are zooming away from us at high speed. The universe is expanding rapidly, as we speak. And this has been going on for some time.

That means that in the past, the universe was much smaller and everything was closer together. In fact, if we rewind time to the very beginning, we discover that the universe started as a single incredibly small, incredibly compact point that just "blew up" many, many years ago (14.5 billion if you are counting).

Scientists call that blowup the Big Bang. It was the point when everything began to exist in a big explosion of energy.

Not only did matter and energy start to exist, but according to Einstein, even time and space began to exist. Before the Big Bang, there was nothing—nothing at all.

No matter to touch, no energy to feel, not even space or time. Wow. It's hard to understand, but that's what scientists tell us.

Now, let's think about that. What caused the Big Bang?

Common sense tells us something must have caused it. We know that things don't randomly appear out of nowhere for no reason (except in cartoons). So the Big Bang must have been caused by something. Can we figure out what?

Well, whatever caused it must have been smart, because the universe we see around us is amazingly beautiful and complex. Nothing stupid could have caused it.

Also, whatever caused it must have been very powerful—powerful enough to bring the whole universe into existence.

Finally, whatever caused it must be *outside* space and time, because space and time did not exist before the Big Bang.

So we need an incredibly smart, incredibly powerful Being who is outside of space and time. And that's exactly how God has usually been defined: an all-wise, all-powerful Creator not bound by time or space.

Looking Down

We just looked up with the help of telescopes. Next, let's look down with the help of microscopes.

If we look closely at the dirt under our feet, we will notice that there are things living in it. Millions of them. Little single-celled creatures. My mom just called them "germs," but scientists might call them "protists."

We put them under a microscope, and at first they look like blobs of Jell-O. But under very high magnification, we discover that each one looks like an amazing little city inside, with thousands of tiny "nanobots" moving around on guide wires, bringing food over here and dumping garbage over there.

It's mind-boggling but true! You can get on YouTube and see animations of it.[1] (There are also some links in the back of this book.)

What amazes me is that these are the *simplest* living things. Even the simplest living cell is swarming with "nanobots" inside and needs them to live. (Scientists call them "molecular machines" and say they're made of proteins.)

Where did they come from? We did not make them. Living things have been around almost since the earth was formed. Yet even today, we don't have the technology to make even the simplest living cell. Even in a lab, it's far beyond our ability to make a living thing from scratch.

So who put the first life on earth? Someone must have, because we know life cannot happen by chance. Chemicals will not organize themselves into the "nanobots of life" by themselves. We've tried to get them to do that. It doesn't work.

So whoever did it had to be smart—smarter than we are, because we couldn't have done it.

And whoever did it must have been very good at controlling nature—much better than we are.

So someone very smart and very good at controlling nature: it sounds like our definition of God once more.

Looking Around

Next, let's look around us. One of the things we notice about nature, everywhere we look, is that things happen in an orderly way. Things fall to the ground very predictably. We call that force gravity. Sound travels at a predictable speed, and so does light. We can put numbers to the speed of sound and the speed of light.

Our world is ordered and predictable because it follows what we call "natural laws." When two pool balls hit each other, we have math formulas that can tell us how fast they will roll away and at what angles.

Now, here is an amazing fact: we have discovered that all the natural laws are at exactly the right setting for life to exist on earth.

Gravity is exactly right: if gravity was even slightly stronger, the whole universe would re-collapse into a black hole, and we would not be alive. If gravity were even slightly weaker, the universe would be nothing but clouds of gas, and we would not be alive. But gravity is exactly right, and here we are.

The speed of light is exactly right. If light were slightly faster, the universe would be too bright and hot for life. If light were slightly slower, the universe would be too dull and cool for life. But light is exactly right, and here we are.

The same holds true for dozens of other natural laws: the forces of electricity and of magnetism, the tiny forces inside atoms, and so on and so on.

Everything is "just right" for life. We live in a Goldilocks world where everything is "just right" for us.

Scientists have a name for this reality. They call it "cosmic fine-tuning." They say the natural laws of the universe are "fine-tuned" for living things. And not just any living things, but especially human beings. Nature seems to have been designed for us human beings. Even atheist scientists admit that this is one of the strongest evidences that there is a God.[2]

Suppose you walked into a new house and were surprised to find that the rooms were painted in your favorite color and that your favorite meal was laid out on the dining room table, the fridge was stocked with your favorite drinks, and the bedroom was decorated with your favorite photos. Wouldn't you suspect someone knew you were coming?

That's how it is with our universe and earth. It's as if someone knew we were coming. The water, the minerals, the temperature, the light, the gravity, the wind, the waves, the tides, the plants—everything is just what we need.

So who set all the laws of nature at exactly the right setting for human life? Common sense tells us it didn't happen by chance. Aliens couldn't have done it, because they weren't around at the Big Bang. In fact, nothing *in* the universe could have set up the laws *of* the universe.

So whoever set the laws of nature must be outside the universe. And must have been very smart, because the laws of nature are amazing and work together in harmony. And must have been powerful too, to put limits on the very forces of nature.

So once more, we are in need of an all-wise, all-powerful Creator outside of time and space. That's the traditional job description of God.

Someone or Something Out There?

But maybe you say,
"Not so quick!
Why does the Creator
have to be God? Maybe
just a 'higher power'
or a 'force' put us here."

So how *do* we know God is Someone rather than something?

I think the answer is pretty simple. When we looked around us, we saw signs of planning.

The universe, with its fine-tuned laws that make human life possible, looks as if it were made just for us.

So whatever made all this must have planned, must have thought ahead.

But "forces" or "powers," like gravity and electricity, don't think or plan. They don't think at all. Only a person can think.

So *whatever* put us here is a *whoever*. It's not a something but a Someone. Not a "higher power" but a "Higher Person."

Looking Inside

Finally, let's look inside ourselves.

Deep inside us, we have this thing we call a conscience. It makes us feel good when we do right, and it nags us when we do wrong. In fact, it makes us feel *guilty* when we've done wrong.

But how does our conscience know what's right or wrong? Or another way to ask this question: what *makes* something right or wrong?

Is it I? Clearly not. It can't be *me* who makes something right or wrong, because my conscience doesn't just agree with whatever I want. Often I want something very badly, but my conscience tells me it is wrong. And no amount of my wanting, wishing, or trying will make right something I know in my heart is wrong. So I'm not the source of right and wrong. Is it everyone around me? Clearly not. A majority vote can't make something wrong into something right. Even if everyone on the planet said it was okay to kill an innocent girl for no reason, that wouldn't make it right. So everyone else is not the source of right and wrong either.

Could it be the universe? Clearly not. The universe is wonderful, but it doesn't think. The stars, planets, water, and wind do the things they do—burn and orbit and splash and blow—but they don't think, care, feel, or choose. But right and wrong always involve choice. So the universe can't be the cause of right and wrong.

So whatever the source of right and wrong is, it's not I, the people around me, or the universe.

And it must be *personal*, because right and wrong only apply to persons who can choose. Something that has no free choice—like a rock, a robot, or a rose—can't do right and wrong. Only persons can, because only persons can choose. So the source of right and wrong can't be impersonal. To be honest, the source has to be a person. Laws need a lawgiver. So our consciences testify to right and wrong. And right and wrong need a Person apart from the universe who is their source. Once more, that sounds like God.

That's what the very smartest atheists have always realized: if there is no God, there is no right or wrong. In the godless world of the famous atheist Richard Dawkins, "There is, at bottom . . . no evil and no good, nothing but blind, pitiless indifference."[3]

But Dawkins is wrong. In the real world, there is both evil and good, both right and wrong. And therefore, there is a God.

Putting It All Together

So this is my point: whether we look up, down, all around, or inside, we see signs that point to God. The evidence is there, if we are open to it.

How about you? Are you open to it? Are you willing to accept the evidence for God?

An Objection

But maybe you have an objection. While we were looking up and down and all around, there was something else you may have noticed: bad stuff.

There is evil in the world. Wars, sickness, crime, and death.

"Don't these prove there is no God?" you might ask. I agree: it's a fair question, one I've struggled with myself.

This is called the problem of evil. Many think evil proves there is no God.

If there were a God, the argument goes, there would be no war, crime, disease, or natural disasters. God is all good and all powerful, so he would prevent anything bad from happening.

But that's not necessarily so.

One possibility could be this: God is not good. I don't believe it myself, but we have to consider that option. Maybe there is a God, but he's not so concerned about us, and he lets these evil things happen. On the other hand, maybe God is good and still lets these things exist.

How could that be?

For one thing, most of the evil isn't God's fault; it's our fault. Wars, murders, crimes are all things *humans* do. The only way God could prevent these things is if he *controlled us*.

But maybe God doesn't want to control us. Maybe he wants us to be free.

But if we are free, God has to put up with our misusing our freedom. And that means other people *do* end up getting hurt.

The only alternative would be to make us into robots who always have to do the right thing.

The problem with robots, however, is that they can't love. They can't love, because they don't have free choice. They can only do what they are programmed to do.

I think God wanted us to be able to love. And that meant we had to be free. But free people can also misuse freedom and do evil.

Let's move on to another idea: maybe the evil is here for us to overcome. If there were nothing for us to struggle against in this world, we would become pretty pathetic people.

Have you ever met someone who has had almost no real pain or suffering in life? Who was born with a so-called silver spoon in his mouth? Who had everything handed to him on a platter?

Now, did you like that person?

Probably not. People who have never had to struggle are often spoiled and shallow.

On the other hand, some of the wisest people I know are people who have had a lot of suffering. Some people have gotten very wise—and very beautiful on the inside—by struggling through adversity. Mother Teresa of Calcutta comes to mind.

For myself, I think that God is good yet allows evil for the reasons above.

God wants us to be free to love each other and to love him. But love can't be forced. For us to *really* love, we have to be free to choose. But the downside is, not everyone chooses love. So we have wars, murders, and crimes.

Yet even these evils serve a purpose. They give us something to struggle against.
They give us a chance to grow up.
To be a hero.
    To show courage.
      To show perseverance.
        To prove our love by self-sacrifice.
          To become better, nobler, more inspiring people.

A world full of shallow, spoiled people who have never suffered and overcome would be a pretty lame world.

It's for these reasons that God can be good and yet allow evil. At least that's how I see it. There's a lot more that could be said. But for now, maybe we can agree that evil doesn't *necessarily* mean there is no God.

Back to the Question of God

So we've looked up and down and all around from
our rock as we hurtle along in space, and we've seen
many things that point to something very smart and
very powerful. What do you say? Are you willing to
accept, for now, that there just might be a God? If so,
do you want to join me for the next question and ask,
"Has this God ever said anything to us?"

1. See the TED talk by Drew Berry, "Animations of Unseeable Biology," https://www.youtube.com/watch?v=WFCvkkDSfIU; and "The Inner Life of the Cell," https://www.youtube.com/watch?v=FzcTgrxMzZk.

2. Atheist Stephen Hawking admits, "The remarkable fact is that the values of these numbers [i.e., the constants of physics] seem to have been very finely adjusted to make possible the development of life," and he concedes that one could accept this as evidence of "a divine purpose in Creation and the choice of the laws of science" by God (*A Brief History of Time* [New York: Bantam Books, 1998], 129, 130).

3. The full quote is "The universe we observe has precisely the properties we should expect if there is, at bottom, no design, no purpose, no evil, no good, nothing but blind, pitiless indifference" (Richard Dawkins, *River Out of Eden: A Darwinian View of Life* [New York: Basic Books, 1995], 133).

Chapter 3

Has God Spoken?

So here we are, hanging out together on this speeding ball of rock we call the earth.

And we are talking about all the Big Questions, the GLUE questions.

And I've just said that nature points to the existence of a Creator, of a God.

If there is a God, then the next question could be "Has this God spoken to us?"

You would think that a God smart enough to design things like the DNA in our cells would be able to communicate with us.

Bill Gates has called DNA a program far more advanced than any software humans have created. Bill Clinton has called it "the language in which God created life."[1]

So the Someone who came up with DNA surely has language ability. Couldn't he find a way to communicate with his creatures?

Any God willing to go through all the trouble of making us, and this whole planet that keeps us alive, would want to tell us something about why he did it.

Wouldn't he?

And maybe he could say something about what our purpose is?

So if it's okay with you, can we at least take a look to see is there any evidence that God *has* spoken to us?

Who Claims That God Has Spoken?

When we talk about God speaking to us, we get into the area of religion.

Of course, there are many religions in the world that claim that God has spoken through some holy man or holy woman.

But most of these are quite small, and almost all their followers come from one country or ethnic group. Examples would be

Judaism for the Jews,
Shintoism among the Japanese,
and Sikhism among Punjabis (Punjab is
in India).

However, if the Creator of the universe has spoken to us, it would seem that the message would spread beyond one nation or group.

It seems more likely that if God has spoken, a lot of people would know about it, and it would become a major worldwide movement.

So let's look at the major world religions to see if any of them make a believable case that God has spoken to humanity.

Surprisingly, there are only four world religions large enough to be considered "major," and these are Buddhism, Hinduism, Islam, and Christianity.

What does each one say about whether God has spoken?

First, Buddhism.

There are about a half billion Buddhists in the world, almost all in different Asian countries.

Buddhism does not claim that God has spoken to us.

Buddhism was founded by Siddhartha Gautama, an Indian holy man who became known as "the Buddha," which means "Enlightened One."

The Buddha did not clearly teach whether there was a God. He was an "agnostic," a person who doesn't know whether God exists.

The Buddha and Buddhism are not concerned with God exactly but rather with escaping the cycles of reincarnation through enlightenment.

So if we are trying to find out about God, that's not a question Buddhism tries to answer.

Second, Hinduism.

Hinduism has about a billion followers, mostly persons who live in or near India or who descend from Indians. It is difficult to separate Hinduism from the Indian culture. Moreover, Hinduism is broken into thousands of different sects, cults, and traditions that often disagree with one another on basic issues. There are Hindu sacred books, but Hindus themselves debate about how to understand them.

Hinduism doesn't have just one God or one idea of God. There are many gods you can worship and pray to, and there are many ways to think about God or the gods.

So if we are looking to see if God has spoken to humanity, Hinduism doesn't look very helpful. At least, it would take a long time to sort through all the different claims and issues. If we need to, we can come back to it after looking at other options.

Third, Islam.

The situation in Islam is much clearer. Over a billion Muslims agree that there is one God, Allah, and that Muhammad was his prophet.

Muslims have a holy book, the Quran, which they believe is God's word to humanity. It was written down by the prophet Muhammad.

If you want to know what God has said, read the Quran. That's the position of Islam.

Fourth, Christianity.

The situation in Christianity is clearer too. Over two billion Christians believe in one God and believe that God's word is contained in the Bible, a collection of books written by holy men over a long period of time.

But there is also something unique about Christianity. Christians believe that God's word is not just a book but a person, Jesus Christ.

For Christians, it is through Jesus Christ that God has spoken to the world.

Curiously, though, Islam also agrees that God spoke through Jesus.

To be sure, Muslims do not believe all the same things about Jesus that Christians do. But they agree that he was a great prophet.

In the Quran, Jesus is mentioned twenty-five times, and the prophet Muhammad, just four times. The Quran says that Jesus was a great prophet. According to the Quran, he cured sick people, raised the dead, ascended to heaven, and will come back one day. The Quran calls him "the word of God" and "the spirit of God." This is more than it says about Muhammad himself, even though Muhammad wrote the Quran.

The Quran even has a special place for Mary, the mother of Jesus. She is the only woman mentioned in the Quran. A whole chapter is devoted to her.

What an amazing testimony! We are looking for evidence that God has spoken to us. We find that the world's two largest religions agree that God has spoken to us through a man named Jesus. Together, these two religions account for about half the population on the globe.

How remarkable!

Earlier, we thought, if God has really spoken, it should have had a big impact.

If God has really spoken, people should know about it.

And, in fact, we discover that half the world's population agrees that there was something special about this man Jesus. He really spoke the words of God; in fact, in some sense, he *is* God's word.

No other figure in human history has this kind of following. No philosopher, prophet, guru, or teacher is recognized by so many. Even many Jewish leaders have been impressed with Jesus.

The most famous modern Jewish philosopher, Martin Buber, said:

From my youth onwards I have found in Jesus my great brother. . . . I am more than ever certain that a great place belongs to him in Israel's history of faith and that this place cannot be described by any of the usual categories.[2]

The most famous Jewish scientist, Albert Einstein, said:

I am a Jew, but I am enthralled by the luminous figure of the Nazarene [Jesus]. . . . No one can read the Gospels without feeling the actual presence of Jesus. His personality pulsates in every word. No myth is filled with such life.[3]

So Christians, Muslims, and many Jews agree: there is something special about this Jesus person.

So if we want to investigate whether God has spoken to the human race, it would be pretty ridiculous to ignore this fellow Jesus and start with Confucius, for example (who, by the way, never claimed to speak for God).

Let's start with the obvious.
Let's start with the elephant in the room.
Let's examine the person who changed the human race so much that the whole world dates the years by counting from his birth.

1. Bill Gates, *The Road Ahead: Completely Revised and Up-to-Date* (New York: Penguin, 1996), 228; Remarks of President Bill Clinton, June 26, 2000, quoted in Francis Collins, *The Language of God: A Scientist Presents Evidence for Belief* (New York: Free Press, 2006), 2.

2. Martin Buber, *Two Types of Faith* (New York: Harper, 1961), 12, 13.

3. *Saturday Evening Post* interview with Albert Einstein, as quoted in Mike McKinley, *Am I Really a Christian?* (Wheaton, IL: Crossway, 2011), 44.

Chapter 4

Has God Spoken through Jesus?

Okay, so who is this guy Jesus? Why do so many people think God has spoken through him?

Four biographies of Jesus were written within a few decades of his death. We call them by the names of their authors: Matthew, Mark, Luke, and John. Matthew and John were part of the original band of students Jesus hung out with for several years. Mark and Luke were friends and helpers of Jesus' original band of students.

These biographies are called "Gospels" by English-speaking Christians.

The word *Gospel* is an old English word meaning "Good News." For Christians, the life of Jesus is "Good News."

Let's give a quick overview of Jesus' life.

He was born and raised in the land of Israel by
his parents, Joseph and Mary, who were poor
descendants of royalty.

Around age thirty, he began to teach and preach in
public.

He gathered students around himself, including twelve
special ones whom he called "apostles," which means
"the sent ones."

He also performed many miracles. Healings were
a specialty of his: he cured blind, lame, and deaf
people, those who were paralyzed, and those who had
epilepsy. He cast out demons from people (exorcisms)
and was able to control nature, such as the weather
and the behavior of animals.[1]

Since he could perform these wonders, it's not
surprising that he gathered a large following.
Eventually, both the Jewish and the Roman leaders
of his day began to see him as a threat to their power.
He was so popular that they feared he might try to
take over the country. So they arrested him on false
charges and killed him by crucifixion—a slow death

in which the person hangs from a tree or a pole by the arms until the chest collapses and the person suffocates.

If that were all that happened to Jesus, we wouldn't be talking about him.

The really interesting part is that a couple of days after his death, his tomb was discovered empty, even though there were guards there.

Then Jesus began appearing and talking with his former students. Many of them—men, women, old and young. For several weeks.

He repeated his basic teachings to them,
taught them more about heaven and God,
and commissioned them to spread the word about
him.

Normally, something like this would sound too
crazy and we would just forget about it. But we have
documents from about a half dozen of Jesus' coworkers and their friends— not only John, Matthew,
Mark, and Luke, as we have already mentioned, but
also Peter and Paul.

They all say they saw Jesus and hung out with him
after his death.

It's hard to believe that they were all lying about this,
because they didn't have any motive. None of them
got anything out of this shtick: not money, public
office, power, drugs, or girls. They just spent their
time traveling and talking about how amazing Jesus
was.

Most were eventually tortured and killed because they
wouldn't shut up about Jesus, which annoyed the
authorities.

Some people who've claimed to be prophets or religious leaders have gotten a lot of money, power, or women out of the deal, and we suspect that was the purpose of their prophet-shtick in the first place.

That explanation won't work with Jesus and his followers. They didn't get any of those things. It's hard to see what their motives were, except that they sincerely believed.

So that's a little bit about the life of Jesus, as written down by his coworkers.

But what was it that Jesus taught?
If he claimed to speak for God, what was his message?

That's the topic of our next chapter.

1. See, for example, the Gospel of Mark 4:35-41; the Gospel of Matthew 8:28-34.

Chapter 5

What Did Jesus Say?

So here we are, talking together as we speed through space on the planet earth.

We've seen that science points to a God and that a huge number of people agree God has spoken through Jesus. And we've reviewed some basic facts about the life of Jesus.

But what did Jesus say to us that is supposed to be from God?

Well, he said *a lot*, but let me boil it down for you to four basics:

Jesus said (1) to repent, (2) to love, (3) to call God "Father," and (4) to believe Jesus is God.

Jesus Said to Repent

According to his biographers, Jesus' basic message to people of his day was "Repent! For the kingdom of God is here!"[1]

To "repent" means to recognize that something you are doing is wrong, to feel sorry for it, and to stop doing it.

When Jesus told the people of his day that they needed to repent, he meant they were doing things that were wrong, and they had to stop.

What was it exactly that they were doing that was wrong? Pretty much the same things that people do today that are wrong and that you and I sometimes do: lying, cheating, stealing, being jealous of each other, speaking ill of each other, ignoring the poor and oppressed, being selfish, being proud, breaking promises, and a thousand other similar things.

The name for wrongdoing often used in the Bible, and by Jesus, is *sin*.

Few people understand what the word *sin* means anymore, so we have to rethink it.

A sin is a wrongdoing that offends God. But to really understand sin, we have to know something about God and what offends him.

Many people think that God has a long list of fun things that he doesn't want human beings to do, and when we do one of these things, he marks it off as a sin. But this is a really messed-up picture.

Jesus taught us not only that God is loving but that God is love itself. God loves us incredibly. What offends him is anything that is not loving.

Things that we do that are not loving toward others, that show a lack of concern or even a hatred of others, are wrong.

That is what sin is: a lack of love.

SIN

A religious teacher once asked Jesus, "What is the most important thing that God wants us to do?"

And Jesus answered, "Love God with everything you have, and love others as much as you love yourself. This is the main message of the holy books."[2]

I think we often miss the connection between God's law, sin, and love.

Many people have heard of the Ten Commandments, for example. They may know some of the commandments: "You shall not kill." "You shall not commit adultery." "You shall not steal." "You shall not lie."

But they may not understand *why* these things are forbidden.
Why they are wrong?
Why are they sin?

It's because they are all unloving deeds.

Killing someone is obviously the opposite of loving the person.

Cheating on your spouse (adultery) is very unloving, very hurtful to the person you are supposed to love more than anyone else in your life.

Stealing a person's belongings is certainly not showing love. Nor is lying, because you ought not trick or fool a person you love.

I've heard major public personalities say that the Ten Commandments are "out of date" or need to be replaced with "more modern guidelines."

Really? It's okay to kill people now? Lie? Steal? Envy?

Maybe people who don't believe in God would object to the first three commandments, which are about God, his name, and a day for worship.

But hopefully we all recognize that the other seven are common sense.[3]

Getting back to Jesus' message: when he preached, "Repent!" he meant that people needed to recognize that many things they were doing were against God's law,
which is the same thing as saying they were unloving and selfish.

Jesus wanted people to recognize their wrongdoing, feel sorrow for it,
and turn away from it.

Jesus Said to Love

Okay, so Jesus said to repent. That means to stop doing what's wrong and unloving. That's a negative command, something we are *not* supposed to be doing. But what is the positive command? What did Jesus say we were supposed *to do?*

We've talked about it already. The answer is obvious: we are supposed to love. Love is supposed to guide all our actions.

There is a lot of confusion about what *love* means nowadays. The band Foreigner sings a song with the refrain, "I wanna know what love is." Tina Turner asks in a song, "What's love got to do, got to do with it? What's love but a secondhand emotion?"

Love is not a secondhand emotion. It is not an emotion at all. Love, as Jesus taught it, is first of all an *action*. It is *doing what's best for the other person.*

Jesus summed up his teaching about loving others with this statement: "Whatever you want other people to do for you, do for them; that sums up the message of the holy books."[4]

From this statement of Jesus, we get what people call "the Golden Rule": "Do to others what you would like them to do to you."

Of course, when we love others, we shouldn't do what's best for them while hating them in our hearts. As much as possible, we should try to have the *feelings* that go along with loving actions—like compassion, concern, and affection. All the same, the core of love is *action*, not *feelings*.

Jesus' best student, a man named John, put it like this:

> If anyone has wealth and sees his friend in need, yet refuses to help him, how can he really have God's love in him? Dear friends, let us not love just with words and talking but with actions, which is true love.[5]

Jesus taught us to love radically. The first person we should love is God. As I mentioned above, when Jesus was asked about the most important thing we need to do in life, he said, "Love God with everything you have: all your heart, your soul, your mind, your strength."[6]

Maybe you wonder, "Why should God want to be loved?"

Isn't that selfish of him? Or maybe arrogant?

We should love God because he loved us first. It's only right to love the people who have shown you love. We love our parents because they gave us life and made sacrifices to feed, clothe, and educate us. It's only right that we should love them.

Well, God has done even more. He gave us our parents. He gave us life. He gave us this world, with all its amazingness. This world, fine-tuned for life, is his gift to us. It's only right that we should be grateful, that we should love him back.

But there is more.

Jesus taught that God is the source of all love, even that he is love itself.

His friend John put it like this:

> He who does not love does not know God; for God is love. . . . God is love, and he who lives in love lives in God, and God lives in him.[7]

When we love God, we love Love itself.

Loving God helps us to love others,
because God is the source of all love.
In fact, without God, we can't love others perfectly.

We need God's help to love other people,
because other people can be just too hard for us to
love on our own.

For example, we all have enemies, people who have
wronged us.
Jesus taught that we even have to love them.

In one of his sermons, Jesus said:

You've heard people say,
"You've got to love your friends and hate your
enemies."
But I say, you have to love your enemies,
do good to those who hate you,
bless those who curse you,
pray for those who mistreat you.

If you love those who love you, what credit is
that to you?
For even swindlers love those who love them.
And if you do good to those who do good to you,
what credit is that to you?
For even criminals do the same.

But if you love your enemies,
you will be children of God,
for God is kind to ungrateful and selfish people.[8]

But who can really love their enemies? It's too much
for a person to handle. That's why Jesus also promised
to give his followers God's love, so that they would
be able to love others even when it was humanly
impossible. We'll come back to this idea later.

Jesus Said to Call God "Father"

I just mentioned Jesus' teaching that if we love our
enemies, we will be like children of God.

That brings up another very important part of Jesus'
teaching. He said that God is our Father.

If you grew up in America or a similar country,
this probably doesn't impress you very much. Since
America is a country founded mostly by Christians,
the idea that God is our loving Father is just in the air.
We have all heard politicians and leaders say things
like, "Let's stop fighting, because we are all God's
children."

However, most people in the world *do not* believe God is a loving father.

Atheists, for example, don't believe there is a God at all, much less that he is a loving father. Whole countries are officially atheist, like China, North Korea, and Cuba. The British writer Richard Dawkins and people like him have made atheism very popular elsewhere too.

Islam teaches that God has no children, and the idea of "children of God" is offensive to Muslims.

Buddhism does not teach that there is a God, much less that he is a loving father.

Other religions might believe in a god or gods that are *fatherlike*.

But Christianity is unique, because Jesus taught that God isn't just *like* a father.

Jesus says: God *is* the real Father. Human dads just imitate him, imperfectly.

But why don't we take a moment to ask, "What is a father?" Many of us grew up without knowing our fathers. Others of us never got along with our fathers or were even hurt by them. So what does Jesus mean by *Father?*

Jesus describes his Father as "perfect" and "merciful."[9] The Father is generous with everyone, even those who hate him.[10] He knows what his children need even before they ask for it.[11] He knows how to give good gifts to his children and is more eager to do so than human fathers.[12] Most of all, he is forgiving. He is ready to forgive his children long before they are ready to ask forgiveness.[13] But he will not forgive children who will not forgive their brothers and sisters.[14]

One day, Jesus' students asked him to teach them to pray. Jesus said:

When you pray, say this:

Our Father who is in heaven,
May your name be holy.
May your kingdom come,

And your will be done,
On earth just as it is in heaven.[15]

This was extremely radical in Jesus' day, as it is in ours.

Today, most people around the world do not think of God as our Father.

Likewise, in Jesus' day, most people did not think of God that way.

Jesus lived among Greeks, Romans, and Jews.

The Greeks and Romans believed in many gods, all of whom behaved badly, running around fighting and sleeping with each other—as in a bad soap opera. No loving father-god there.

The Jews had just a few prophets who had spoken of God as father on several occasions, but it was very rare. In Jesus' first recorded sermon alone, he spoke of God as our Father more than all the Jewish prophets before him combined!

If anyone in the world today thinks of God as
their Father,
it is largely because of the teaching of Jesus.
It is a key idea he gave to world culture.

But to be exact, Jesus said we all have the *potential* to
be God's children.
To realize that potential, there are some things we
have to do.
One of them is to love, as we've discussed.
But there are a few other things too, which we can
come back to later.

Jesus Said He Was God

We've decided to investigate whether Jesus really
spoke to us on behalf of God.
And so far, we've seen that Jesus told us, in God's
name,
that we have to repent and to love
and that God is a loving Father to human beings.

Sounds good so far. In fact, it's hard to see what's
offensive about all that. It makes us wonder, "If that's
all he taught, how did he get himself killed?" Why

would the government execute a nice guy who went around talking about love?

Here's where we get to the controversial part: What made people upset was that Jesus claimed he was God.

He knew that it would be hard for people to swallow. How can a man be God? So he did not begin by standing on street corners telling everyone, "Hey, I'm God! Worship me!"

Instead, he spent a long time dropping hints and letting people figure it out for themselves. He would do things that only God can do and then let people think about it.

For example, Jesus would often free people from demons, even the most powerful ones. That's something only God can do. People were shocked and wondered, "Who is this guy?"

Again, he cured diseases and sicknesses of every kind. He would even forgive sins. One time some men brought him a paralyzed man on a stretcher, and Jesus just told him, "My son, your sins are forgiven." Only God can forgive sin, and people there realized that. They grumbled to each other, "Who is this guy who acts as if he can forgive people's sins? Only God can do that!" But to prove that he really did have that Godlike power, Jesus healed the man's paralysis too, and the man stood up and walked away.[16]

Again, Jesus was on a lake in a boat with his students in the middle of the night, and a storm was about to sink them. His students woke Jesus up, since he was sleeping in the back of the boat. When he realized what was going on, Jesus just told the winds and waves to calm down, and they did. His students were shocked, and they said to each other, "Who is this guy who even commands the winds and waves?" They knew that only God could control the weather.[17]

But in time, Jesus spoke more openly about being God. One time, while teaching a large group of Jews, Jesus said he had the power to give eternal life to his followers. Not only that, but after teaching about God as Father, he claimed: "I and the Father are one." The crowd tried to kill him for claiming to be God, but he got away.[18]

The night before he was finally arrested by the authorities, Jesus was sharing dinner with his students. He was talking to them about God, the loving Father. One of his students, Philip, asked him, "Show us the Father, and that will be enough for us."

Jesus replied, "Have I been with you so long, and you don't know me, Philip? He who has seen me has seen the Father. How can you say, 'Show us the Father?' I am in the Father, and the Father is in me."[19]

In this way, he taught that he, Jesus, was equal to the Father, the maker of all things.

Finally, we can mention something that happened after Jesus rose from the dead. One of his students, Thomas, did not believe that he had risen, even though others had seen Jesus. "Unless I see him for myself and examine his body, I won't believe," Thomas said. So Jesus came and paid a visit to Thomas and let him examine his body, the wounds he had gotten when he was tortured and killed. Thomas was amazed and dropped to his knees. "You are my master and my God!" Thomas said to Jesus. Jesus did not correct Thomas and say, "You've got it all wrong.

I'm not God!" Instead, he told Thomas, "You are blessed because you have seen and believe. Even more blessed are those who do not see and still believe."[20]

Believe what? Obviously, that Jesus is God.

Summing Up What Jesus Said

No one in all of human history has convinced more people that he spoke for God than Jesus Christ. Almost half the population of the earth says they believe that he was God's special messenger in some way.

What was this message he brought from God? I summed it up in four points: he said to repent, to love, to believe in God as Father, and to believe in himself as God.

Of course, it was that last point that gave people the most problems.

Jesus is the only major religious teacher ever to claim he was God.
Muhammad did not claim to be God.

Buddha did not claim there even was a God.
Confucius did not claim to be God.
Nor did Zoroaster, Guru Nanak, Plato, or any other
founder of a major religion or philosophy.

Many people have pointed out that there are only
four options with Jesus:

either he was lying,
he was a lunatic,
he was a legend,
or he really is the Lord God.

Liar, Liar, Pants on Fire!

He could have been lying about himself being God.

The problem is, he doesn't come off as a liar when
you read the rest of his life and teachings.

For one thing, he taught the highest moral standards of any world religious teacher or philosopher. Socrates, Plato, Confucius, Zoroaster, Buddha, and others taught many good moral truths. But none of them raised the bar so high as to say we should love even our enemies. And that's just one example. It's a little hard to believe that the world's greatest moral teacher was lying about himself the whole time.

Second, it's hard to see what Jesus would get out of lying. Most liars have a motivation. They lie to get power, pleasure, or profit. Some religious leaders ended up with plenty of wives, money, and power. That seems suspicious. They may have been lying for their own gain.

But Jesus got nothing. He never married, and he died penniless. On more than one occasion, crowds tried to take him and make him king by force, but he ran away![21] He showed no interest in gathering power, pleasure, or profit. So what would motivate him to lie about being God, especially since it would get him killed?

Crazy Man!

Maybe Jesus was a lunatic. Many crazy people have thought they were God.

The only problem is, such crazy people are usually not great moral teachers.
Also, genuinely crazy people are usually dysfunctional. They have too many quirks and oddities to be good leaders and inspire confidence among large groups of people.

Even during his lifetime, some of Jesus' listeners accused him of being crazy. "This man has a demon, and he's mad. Why are you listening to him?" they said to the crowds. But the majority of Jesus' listeners disagreed: "This man doesn't speak like someone demon possessed," they pointed out. "Besides, can a demon-possessed man perform healings like curing blindness?"[22]

King Arthur and Paul Bunyan!

Maybe Jesus was a legend.

Maybe people just made up stories about a magical hero who claimed he was God and worked healings.

This explanation will not work, because we have four biographies of him written by people who lived at the same time.

Plus, there are lengthy references to him by others, like Paul, the early missionary (who knew him after his resurrection), and the most important historian of the time, a man named Joseph Flavius (usually called Josephus).

We have more information, from more people, about the life of Jesus than about almost any other ancient figure. If we are going to start calling Jesus a legend, are we going to do the same with Socrates? Confucius? Cleopatra? Alexander the Great?

But maybe Jesus' *calling himself God* is just a legend. Maybe people made that up later.

The only problem is, all the biographers of Jesus, who lived within his lifetime, believed he claimed to be God. All his early followers, like Paul the missionary, believed it too. This was no legend that grew up hundreds of years later. If Jesus didn't claim to be God, it's amazing that all of his close followers believed that he did.[23]

In fact, we'd have to say that Jesus was a massive failure as a teacher. The world's most famous religious teacher was the worst teacher ever. Because somehow all his students got the idea that he claimed he was God, even though he never did.

Was He Really God?

So it's hard to write Jesus off as a liar, a lunatic, or just a legend. Could he be the Lord God?
But it's impossible for a man to be God! Agreed.
But is it impossible for God to become a man? I don't think so. How could we know that it's impossible?

Years ago, if you told someone all the matter and energy in the universe was once squeezed into the size of a pinhead, people would have said you were crazy.

Now they teach that in schools. It's called the Big Bang theory.

Years ago, if you told someone that the earth was really a ball of rock hurtling through space at a thousand miles an hour, folks would laugh. That's impossible. Everyone would fall off if we were moving that fast.

Now they teach that in schools. It's called the solar system.

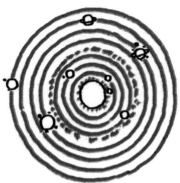

So many things we've thought were "impossible" turned out to be true.

So when someone says that God's becoming a man is "inconceivable," it makes me think of that line from *The Princess Bride:*

"You keep using that word. I do not think it means what you think it means."

Big Claims Need Big Proof

Of course, it's reasonable to expect some kind of proof when someone makes outlandish claims.

If a scientist claimed he found the cure for cancer, you'd want to see his lab results.

If a stranger claimed to shoot hoops better than Lebron James, you'd want to see him play.

So if Jesus claimed to be God, it's okay to expect him to show some kind of proof to back up his big talk.

Jesus' big talk was that we should repent, love, accept God as Father, and believe him to be God.

We'll look at his big deeds in the next chapter.

1. See the Gospel of Mark 1:15.

2. See the Gospel of Matthew 22:36-40. I have simplified the full quote, which is as follows: "Teacher, which is the great commandment in the law?" And he said to him, "You shall love the Lord your God with all your heart, and with all your soul, and with all your mind. This is the great and first commandment. And a second is like it, You shall love your neighbor as yourself. On these two commandments depend all the law and the prophets."

3. The Ten Commandments are
    1. You shall have no other gods besides me.
    2. You shall not misuse the name of God.

3. Keep the sabbath day holy.
4. Honor your father and mother.
5. You shall not kill.
6. You shall not commit adultery.
7. You shall not steal.
8. You shall not lie.
9. You shall not covet your neighbor's spouse.
10. You shall not covet your neighbor's property.
See the Book of Deuteronomy 5:6-21.

4. See the Gospel of Matthew 7:12: "So whatever you wish that men would do to you, do so to them; for this is the law and the prophets." The "law and the prophets" were the holy books of the Jews, what Christians now call the Old Testament.

5. See the First Letter of John 3:17-18. I am simplifying the language. Here is the full quote: "But if any one has the world's goods and sees his brother in need, yet closes his heart against him, how does God's love abide in him? Little children, let us not love in word or speech but in deed and in truth."

6. See the Gospel of Matthew 22:36-37 and the Gospel of Mark 12:28-30.

7. See the First Letter of John 4:8, 16.

8. See the Gospel of Matthew 5:43-48; the Gospel of Luke 6:27-35. Luke 6:35 reads: "But love your enemies, and do good, and lend, expecting nothing in return; and your reward will be great, and you will be sons of the Most High; for he is kind to the ungrateful and the selfish."

9. See the Gospel of Matthew 5:48 and the Gospel of Luke 6:36.

10. See the Gospel of Matthew 5:45.

11. See the Gospel of Matthew 6:8, 32.

12. See the Gospel of Matthew 7:11.

13. See the Gospel of Luke 15:11-32.

14. See the Gospel of Matthew 6:14-15.

15. See the Gospel of Matthew 6:10-11.

16. The full story may be found in the Gospel of Mark 2:1-12.

17. The full story may be found in the Gospel of Mark 4:35-41.

18. See the Gospel of John 10:22-39.

19. The full account is in the Gospel of John 14:8-11.

20. For this account, see the Gospel of John 20:24-29.

21. See the Gospel of John 6:15.

22. See the Gospel of John 10:19-21.

23. For a full discussion of Jesus' claims to be God, see the book by Brant Pitre, *The Case for Jesus: The Biblical and Historical Evidence for Christ* (New York: Image, 2016).

Chapter 6

What Did Jesus Do?

A few years ago, it was a fad to wear a wristband with the letters "WWJD," meaning "What would Jesus do?"

I suppose it was a good thing, meant to remind people to try to imitate Jesus.

The problem is, many times when I asked myself, "What would Jesus do?" the answer I got was "Work a miracle!"

And I can't work miracles.

But that's what Jesus was famous for doing.

All the biographies of Jesus record him performing wonders.[1]

Even the Jewish historian of the time, known as Josephus, wrote a description of him in one of his books: "Now there was about this time Jesus, a wise man . . . [and] a doer of wonderful works."[2]

There are legends of many persons working miracles in ancient times, but usually they are set "a long time ago in a place far, far away."

Jesus' miracles are different. His biographers give specific locations, details about the persons healed, sometimes their names and those of witnesses, and dates within a few years. It's possible to go to Israel and find the locations, to stand within a few yards of the places where Jesus healed and cast out demons.

He didn't just heal people with backaches or do similar hard-to-prove healings that could just be psychological. He cured deaf people, the blind, the paralyzed, and the epileptic, and he even raised the dead, who were about to be buried or were already buried. This is why the authorities were scared of him and the crowds wanted to make him king.

But the biggest miracle about Jesus was that he died and rose again. His biographers spend about half their time discussing the last week of his life. That's when he went to Jerusalem, taught in the temple, ate the Jewish Passover with his students, and was arrested, tortured, tried, and killed. As shown in movies like *The Passion of the Christ*, the Romans beat Jesus almost to death and then nailed him to a cross, where his body weight hung on his arms. After a few hours, his chest collapsed from weakness and he suffocated. That's how crucifixion works. For good measure, they stabbed a spear in his side to make sure he was dead. Then his friends took his body down and placed it in a tomb.

A few days later, he started appearing alive to his students, which completely floored them.

Why did the people closest to Jesus talk so much about his death and resurrection? We have to go into that a little bit to understand it.

Why Did He Have to Die?

All of Jesus' biographers insist that he knew early on he was going to be killed by the authorities. He told his students ahead of time that it was going to happen and that it was part of his mission. In fact, it was why God sent him. As Jesus said on one occasion, "I came not to be served but to serve, and to give my life as a ransom for many."[3]

Now, that is truly odd. No other religious founder or philosopher claimed that he had come to die. Muhammad fought to kill his enemies, not be killed by them. Buddha didn't come to die but to be enlightened. Confucius, Zoroaster, Plato, and many other gurus saw their mission as teaching, not dying. Even Socrates, who died by suicide, didn't see dying as his life's mission. Jesus is the unique world teacher with a "death wish."

Was Jesus crazy? Let's try to understand him before making that harsh judgment. Jesus was a Jew, and to understand him we need to know something about the ancient Jewish prophets and what they said about the history of the human race.

According to the Jewish prophets, God made the first human couple and put them on earth in a place of perfect peace. However, they didn't love God or trust him. They sinned, which means they acted selfishly.

Sadly, this habit of turning away from God and acting selfishly was passed on to all their descendants. We see this in our own lives. If we are honest, we know that we often do not love others. We put ourselves first in a thousand different ways. The Jewish prophets called this selfishness "sin." The early missionary Paul put it like this: "Every one of us has sinned and fallen short of God's perfection."[4]

Paul also said this: "The wages of sin is death."[5] What did he mean? Simple: sin leads to death.

Why? Because God is an angry master in the sky waiting to zap us when we break one of his laws? No.

It's because God is the source of love and life. To sin is to turn away from God. If you turn away from the source of life, how can you live? It's like refusing to drink. It leads to death. It's not that God doesn't want you to live. It's that you are refusing the love and life he is sending your way.

What kind of death are we talking about? At one level, the death of our bodies. Our sin has bad effects on our bodies over time. According to the Jewish prophets, our sin is the deep reason why our bodies die.[6]

But we are not just body; we are also soul. The soul also dies. This is a more serious death. By death of the soul, we don't mean the soul is destroyed. We mean it is cut off from God, the source of life. Being cut off like this is still an existence, but it's hard to call it "life." The Bible calls it "the second death" or "hell."

The ancient Jews knew that when they turned away from God, it led to death. So their prophets told them, when you sin, bring an animal to God, and kill the animal as a sacrifice for your sin.[7] This symbolized that sin led to death. When a person sins, he or she should die because of their turn away from the source of life. The animal took the place of the person. However, the animal sacrifice was just a symbol. An animal cannot pay the price for human sin.

We have all sinned many times. We have often rejected God, who is love. How can the damage from all these sins be undone, so that our souls can live with God, and even our bodies too?

Jesus claimed he had a solution. He would die in our place.

"I have come to give my life as a ransom for many," he said.[8]

"I am the good Shepherd who lays down his life for his sheep," he said, comparing himself to a shepherd who would rather die than let his sheep be harmed.[9]

Jesus' closest friends compared him to the ancient lambs that the Jews would sacrifice in place of themselves. Jesus' cousin John the Baptist called him "the Lamb of God, who takes away the sin of the world."[10] The ancient Jews would place their hands on the heads of lambs to be sacrificed.

This symbolized placing their sin and guilt on the lamb. The lamb died in their place. But that was just symbolic. An animal can't do that. But a man who is also God, the rightful king of humanity, can do it.

We could compare Jesus to a king of a nation that is guilty of some great offense. The king offers to suffer the punishment on behalf of all his people. The ancient prophet Isaiah spoke about him in advance: "We have all gone astray like sheep, and God has laid all our guilt on him."[11]

Paul put it this way: "God showed his love for us by this: while we were still sinners, Jesus Christ died for us."[12]

God is love, and God loves even to the point of death. We can describe Jesus' death on the cross as a kind of "payment" for our sins. We can call it Jesus' "taking our punishment" on himself. It is those things, but it's more. It also proves how extreme God's love for us is—to the point of death.

Many Christians wear a crucifix around their necks or put one up in their homes or churches. The crucifix is a cross with Jesus' body on it.

It's not morbid or sad. It's a sign of God's love. When I look at a crucifix, I think: "This is my God. He loves me so much that he would become a man like me and suffer the death that I deserve—for me."

Why do I deserve death? Because so many times I've turned away from Life, which is God. You can't turn away from Life without experiencing death.

And what is death? It's separation from God, who is Life.

We see Jesus experiencing this on the cross.

On the cross, Jesus cried out, "My God, my God, why have you abandoned me?"[13]

This is a mystery. Jesus is God. Yet in some sense, he is going through a separation from God the Father—a separation we call death.

Since Jesus was separated from God for us, we do not have to go through that experience ourselves. Our sins can be forgiven. As Jesus said on the night before he was arrested, "My blood is poured out for many for the forgiveness of sins."[14] Again, his best student, John, later wrote, "He is the way of forgiveness for our sins, and not for ours only, but for the sins of the whole world."[15]

Forgiveness of our sins means all our "turnings away" are healed. We can "turn toward" God. His love and life will flow to us!

Now we can sum up what we've learned about Jesus' death.

Jesus told his friends that he had come to die. He described it as "giving his life as a ransom for many," as "laying down his life for his sheep," and as "pouring out his blood for the forgiveness of sins."[16] His cousin called him "the Lamb of God who takes away the sins of the world," using the image of the Jewish sacrifices.

Jesus and his closest friends explained that his death was on our behalf. He suffered the consequence of sin, of turning away from God, so that we could be saved from that consequence. *If we accept his offer*, our souls will not be separated from God, and even our bodies will one day be given life again. Jesus promised us eternal life not as disembodied souls but as resurrected persons with bodies.[17] Our bodies will be changed, but they will still be ours—just like Jesus' body after his resurrection.[18]

Because, after all, Jesus didn't stay dead. Three days later, he got up and left his tomb.

The Resurrection

As we said before, the biggest miracle about Jesus was
his rising from the dead. This is yet another thing that
makes him different from every other religious leader
and philosopher in the world. None of them rose
from the dead, nor did their followers claim they did.

Of course, there are myths and legends of people
coming back from the dead. But Jesus' resurrection
was no myth or legend. The women closest to Jesus
went to his tomb a day or two after his death to wash
his corpse. But they couldn't find it. They panicked
and went to tell his students. His students ran to the
tomb and couldn't find his body either. Then Jesus
started appearing to people.

One of the first people to write about Jesus'
appearances was Paul the missionary. About a decade
after Jesus rose from the dead, Paul wrote to a church
in Greece:

> For I handed on to you as most important what I also
> accepted, that Christ died for our sins as predicted
> in the writings of the prophets, that he was buried,

that he was raised on the third day as predicted in the writings of the prophets, and that he appeared to Peter, then to the Twelve (the apostles). Then he appeared to more than five hundred of his followers at one time, most of whom are still alive, though some have died. Then he appeared to James, then to all of his students. Last of all, like to one born at the wrong time, he appeared also to me.[19]

Paul just mentions the most important appearances that he can remember. Besides what Paul mentions, Jesus also appeared several times to his women followers, as recorded by his biographers.[20]

It's amazing that Paul could make such a bold claim, in a public letter, while most of the people he mentioned were still alive. Anyone who doubted Paul's honesty could check with some of the many people he referred to.

Sometimes dead people have appeared to the living in dreams or visions, or folks have caught glimpses of deceased friends out of the corner of their eye.

But Jesus' appearances weren't like this. He appeared to groups of people, held conversations, and ate meals. In fact, he made a point of eating with people after his resurrection. That proved he wasn't a ghost or a vision.[21]

The authorities hated these reports of Jesus rising from the dead. But the reports should have been easy to disprove. The authorities knew where Jesus' tomb was. They had placed guards there. All they had to do was show the body to the public. But they couldn't, because the body wasn't there. Jesus had left the tomb, even though it was under guard.[22]

If Jesus didn't rise from the dead, he pulled off something almost as miraculous. He managed, somehow, to convince all of his relatives, students, followers, and even a few enemies (like Paul) that he was still alive. In fact, most of these people went on to get killed by the authorities for insisting that Jesus was alive.

People rarely let themselves be killed for something they know is a lie. Usually they walk it back when they realize their story is getting them in major trouble. But none of Jesus' students or associates ever walked back their claims about his being alive, even though almost all ended up tortured and killed.

What Does It Mean?

But what does the resurrection mean? Is it just a curious case for the record books: the only human being known to come back from the dead?

No, it's much more than that. Jesus had told his students on several occasions that he would be killed and later rise from the dead. They didn't understand what he was talking about. Some of his students, like Peter, even gave him pushback and told him he should stop talking about his death. But the fact that Jesus predicted his resurrection, and made good on it, proves that he was not an ordinary person. Supernatural power was at work in him.

The resurrection was an act of God, proving Jesus to be truthful. Anyone who predicts his own rising from the dead and makes good on it has to be taken seriously.

After his resurrection, Jesus accepted worship from his students, who acknowledged him as the Son of God, even God himself.[23] That would be unbelievable arrogance unless he really was God.

For my part, I believe he really is.

1. All four Gospels are filled with miracle stories. The apostle Paul speaks often of the miracle of Jesus' rising from the dead: see his Letter to the Romans 1:4; 8:11; 10:9; First Letter to the Thessalonians 4:14; Second Letter to Timothy 2:8.

2. The greatest Jewish historian of the time of Jesus went by the name Flavius Josephus. He was a retired Jewish army general and scholar who was adopted by the Roman emperor. He wrote a history of the Jews called *The Antiquities of the Jews*, and he describes Jesus in book 18, chapter 3, section 3: "Now there was about this time Jesus, a wise man, if it be lawful to call him a man, for he was a doer of wonderful works, a teacher of such men as receive the truth with pleasure. He drew over to him both many of the Jews, and many of the Gentiles. He was the Christ; and when Pilate, at the suggestion of the principal men amongst us, had condemned him to the cross, those that loved him at the first did not forsake him; for he appeared to them alive again the third day; as the divine prophets had foretold these and ten thousand other wonderful things concerning him. And the tribe of Christians, so named from him, are not extinct at this day."

3. See the Gospel of Mark 10:45.

4. Paul's Epistle to the Romans 3:23.

5. Paul's Epistle to the Romans 6:23.

6. See, for example, Ezekiel 33:10-16.

7. See the Book of Leviticus, chapter 5.

8. See the Gospel of Mark 10:45.

9. See the Gospel of John 10:11.

10. The Gospel of John 1:29.

11. See the Book of the Prophet Isaiah 53:6.

12. See the Epistle to the Romans 5:8.

13. See the Gospel of Matthew 27:46.

14. See the Gospel of Matthew 26:28. The full verse is "For this is my blood of the covenant, which is poured out for many for the forgiveness of sins."

15. See the First Letter of John 2:2.

16. See the Gospel of Mark 10:45; the Gospel of John 10:11; the Gospel of Matthew 26:28.

17. See the Gospel of John 6:40, 44, 54.

18. See the First Epistle of St. Paul to the Corinthians 15.

19. See the First Epistle of St. Paul to the Corinthians 15:3-8.

20. See the Gospel of Matthew, chapter 28; the Gospel of Mark, chapter 16; the Gospel of Luke, chapter 24; and the Gospel of John, chapter 20.

21. See the Gospel of Luke 24:42-43; the Gospel of John 21:4-14; the Acts of the Apostles 10:41.

22. See the Gospel of Matthew 27:62-66.

23. See the Gospel of John 20:26-29.

Chapter 7

Is Jesus a Second God?

I'm sure you're asking at this point, if you haven't already:

"What gives? Jesus taught that God is our Father but also that he himself is God?"

"On the cross, he's separated from God for our sake, yet he really is God?"

"He prays to God as his own Father but lets his followers worship him as God?"

All this makes Jesus and his followers sound pretty crazy.

In order to understand, we have to talk about what Christians call the Trinity.

Jesus taught that there is only one God. At the same time, he taught his students to recognize three persons as God: God the Father, Jesus himself, and God's Spirit. Christians call them God the Father, God the Son, and God the Holy Spirit.

Three persons, one God.

How can this be? One of the best explanations I've heard is the following: with God there is one *what* and three *who*s. What is God? God is just God. But who is God? God is the Father, Son, and Spirit.

This seems impossible, but actually, we see similar puzzles in science.

In the science of the very small, called "quantum physics," we see all kinds of mysterious things.

The tiny basic particles that make up all matter can actually be in more than one location at the same time.

The basic particle of light, called a "photon," acts like both a bullet of matter and a wave of radiation.

How can something be both a hard object and a wave at the same time?

That's the wild world of the very small. These things were first discovered in the early 1900s. Scientists didn't believe it at first. It took decades for people like Einstein to accept the fact that at the smallest level, things defy our common sense.

Could it be that the creator of amazing things, like light particles, is himself amazing?

If light can be both a particle and a wave, could Jesus be both man and God?

If an electron can be in multiple locations at once, could God be Father, Son, and Spirit at the same time?

I'm not saying that the Holy Trinity is exactly like these tiny particles, of course.

I'm just saying that the God who created this surprising world might himself be surprising.

At least we should be open to it.

God Is Love

To me, it makes sense that God is three persons with one nature.

You and I are just one person with one nature. It would actually be surprising if God were no different. Shouldn't God be kind of unique?

To me, this all makes sense when we think of God as love.

Love needs someone else to love. If Love is just one person, all Love can do is love itself. But self-love is a pretty low form of love. It might not be love at all. It might just be selfishness.

If God was just one person, then before the world began, all he could do was love himself.

Does that mean that God had to make us to have someone to love? That would mean God was pretty inadequate. He would need his own creatures in order to become perfect. That almost seems like a contradiction. Isn't God supposed to be perfect by himself?

But if God is more than one person, he has always had another to love.

Christians have thought of it like this:

God the Father loves God the Son.

And God the Son loves the Father back.

And the love that they share is the Holy Spirit.

So God is a circle of family love that is always in motion. Love is always being given and being received.

That sounds more like true love. True love is moving, not still. Dynamic, not static. True love gives itself away. True love shares itself and is not self-centered.

I truly believe that if God is love, then God also has to be more than one person in himself.

A single-person God can only love himself, which is lame.

A multi-person God can love the other person, which is beautiful.

We believe God is a circle of self-giving love, and his love overflows from himself. He wants to welcome his creatures into his self-circle of love.

That's you and I.

When we follow the self-giving example of Jesus who gave himself away to the point of death, we learn to love like God.

We become Godlike, because God is self-giving love.

That's why the crucifix is so powerful for me.

When I look at Jesus dying on the cross, I think to myself:

"That is God. God is self-giving love. That is what God is and what it means to be God and be like God."

And that's a different thought than you would find in atheism or in other religions and philosophies. This is a Jesus difference.

Knowing *About* God versus *Knowing* God

Since we are on the topic of love, this is a good place for us to make an important point: because God is love, he wants you to *know* him, not just *know about* him.

In this book, we've used logic, reason, and even scientific evidence to talk about God's existence. All that is important and has its place. But in the end, God is not just a truth or a formula to be believed, like 2 + 2 = 4 or $E=mc^2$.

In the end, God is a person to be loved, a person who already loves you.

We can encounter God. We can experience him. He wants us to.

Although reason and logic are very important, few people end up coming to God for reason and logic alone.

I have a friend who is a professor, who is super-intelligent and an expert in philosophy. His students love his classes. I go to him when I have big questions I can't answer.

My friend is a believer, a man who prays. But my friend, smart though he is, didn't come to trust in God because of logic. He came to believe in God because he met God in a very personal way.

You see, when he was in his twenties, my friend was a big fan of a certain notorious rock band, and he did nothing but follow them around the country on their tours, selling drugs on the side to make ends meet. When his drug habit got out of control, he became scared. Not knowing what to do, he went back to the prayers he had learned as a child and asked Jesus to come and help him. That prayer was answered. He felt the presence of Jesus entering his life, giving him the strength to make a break with drugs. He made a radical change of direction, enrolled in school, began to study theology and philosophy, and now makes his living teaching. Today you'd never guess what his background was.

That's the way it is with many who follow God. It's usually not just reasons but experiences of God that have changed their lives.

Of course, not everyone's story is so dramatic. I've never been under the influence of drugs, but there was a time in my life when I bottomed out and became clinically depressed. I was convinced that God wanted to destroy me—a crazy idea, I know, but I became obsessed with it. This went on for months, and I could hardly function, hardly make it through each day. I don't know what would have happened to me if it weren't for an old pastor of mine. Desperate, I went to see him and told him my whole struggle. After listening to all of it, he just said something simple:

"John, God doesn't hate you. He loves you."

That was it. I know it doesn't sound like much. It sounds trite, like something from Sunday school. But that's all it took, coming from this man who I knew was so good and so sincere. When he spoke those words, it was as if a spiritual and emotional dam broke loose. I felt a wave of God's love wash over me, and I just broke down. Then we talked some more. When I left his office, I was different. I knew I had experienced God. It wasn't the first or the last time I experienced him, but I share it with you because it was life changing.

So it is important to think about God, to have reasons, and to use logic. Evidence is also important. But let's also "keep it real," as they say. God is not just an idea or a principle but someone we can know personally, someone we can have a relationship with, someone we can love and whose love we can experience.

Let's keep that in mind as we go back to talking about Jesus, this man who rose from the dead.

Chapter 8

Do I Have to Decide about Jesus?

Okay, so what if all this really is true?

Maybe you're thinking:

"Does it make any difference? Maybe Jesus *is* God and rose from the dead. Can I go back to living my life now? I need to do some laundry and study for a big exam tomorrow."

Actually, you and I *can't* just walk away from all this.

We have to make a decision. We have to say either, "This is false, and I ignore it," or, "This is true, and I accept it."

One of the problems about Jesus is that you have to make a decision about him.

Even not deciding is a decision. Jesus once said, "He who is not with me is against me."[1] If his claims are true, we should worship him as God. If his claims are false, we should oppose his whole false agenda. There's not much middle ground.

So we have to make a decision, yes or no, about Jesus.

This decision may make a big difference in how we live in this life and where we live in the life to come. Because Jesus taught that after this life, there will be a judgment of all people. This judgment has two outcomes: either heaven or hell.

Lots of people are uncomfortable with the idea of a final judgment. I get that. Who wants to be judged?

Maybe it would be nicer to believe in a world where there was no judgment—one where everyone goes to heaven.

But would we really want to live in a world where there was no final punishment for evil or reward for good? Where Hitler and Mother Teresa of Calcutta ended up in the same place? I'm not sure we would like a world like that.

For one thing, it would suck all the meaning out of life. Whether you killed and abused millions of people or gave up your life to help the poor, it would make no difference. Everyone's fate would be the same. So why try?

Second, it just doesn't seem right. People really do very evil things. They abuse and kill others and even laugh and mock the people they abuse. If God is good, he has to bring these people to justice.

On the other hand, there are people who make great sacrifices for love. There are those who were killed while trying to save Jews from the Nazis, for example. A good God would honor those people for their acts of love.

Otherwise, the world would seem very unfair. Our sense of right and wrong seems to demand a final judgment, where evil is brought to justice and good is rewarded.

But what about heaven and hell? What are these places like? Could a good God ever send anyone to hell?

To answer these questions, we have to return to the truth that God is love.

Heaven, Hell, and the Love of God

As we saw before, Jesus' best student, John, once summed up one of Jesus' major teachings by saying, "God is love." [2]

The highest love is the gift of oneself to another person. We honor heroes who died protecting their family and country. They loved others more than themselves. We can say they gave themselves for others.

God is perfect self-giving love. As mentioned earlier, Christians often wear a crucifix or hang one in their homes. The crucifix shows Jesus, who is God, giving himself for the whole world. Even to the point of death. Christians believe God gives himself totally, and that's the highest kind of love.

Heaven is a place of self-giving love. All the people in heaven have gotten past selfishness. God gives himself to them, and they give themselves to God. There is no longer any impatience or unkindness or arrogance or rudeness. No one is insisting on his or her own way, no one is being irritable or resentful. No one is lying. There is no longer any pride.

The problem is, not everyone is going to like heaven.

The perfect gift of self in love is more than a lot of people can handle. Especially those who've spent their lives focused on themselves.

Every sin is an act of selfishness. When we lie, cheat, or steal, what we do is choose our own self over other people. Sin is the opposite of love.

When you've spent your life choosing yourself over God and others, it's not possible to suddenly switch after death and become the loving kind of person who can handle heaven.

On judgment day, many people will not even find heaven attractive. God's presence will make them uncomfortable or even pained. It hurts to be in the presence of perfect love when all your life you've been doing the opposite of love. Giving yourself away hurts when you're not used to it, when you've been trying to avoid it your whole life.

God has a place for people who find heaven uncomfortable. A place for those who can't handle the selflessness that perfect love requires. We call that place hell.

Hell is a place for those who can't give themselves away, who can't handle the truth about themselves and what they've done, who can't be transparent or humble. In hell, you don't have to love as God loves. You don't have to be exposed to God's truth and his love. You can keep yourself and have yourself for all eternity.

The Bible sometimes describes hell as an outer darkness and sometimes as a lake of fire.[3] Frankly, I'm not sure if that's supposed to be literal or not. In any case, both those things sound like good descriptions of what it would be like to be wrapped up in yourself forever.

Jesus describes hell as a place where God sends people who do evil.[4] But hell is also a place that people choose. They choose it through their everyday actions all their life long. We shape ourselves by our choices and actions. By the day of our death, we've shaped ourselves into either the kind of people who can choose and enjoy heaven or the kind who would prefer to be in hell.

God can't send everyone to heaven, because he can't make people love. Love is always a free choice. It can't be forced—else it isn't love. Not everyone will choose Love, which is God himself. Love can be painful, because it involves giving ourselves away. Not everyone wants to do that, and God will not force people. In his mercy, he has a safe place for them, where they can choose themselves forever.

One writer has described hell as a room locked—from the inside.[5]

That's how a good God can send someone to hell. A good and loving God will not make us love him or love each other. Nor will he force anyone to choose love. Yet if you can't choose love, heaven is perfectly painful, because heaven is nothing but love. So hell is the second option to avoid the "pain" of heaven.

Judged by Love

If it's okay, let's back up to judgment.

Jesus taught that there would be a judgment of all people one day and that he would be the judge.

But what are we going to be judged on? You can probably guess: love.

There is a wrong idea out there that the Bible says you will go to heaven provided you "believe" in Jesus. I've heard both Christians and atheists make that claim.

That's actually not what the Bible teaches, and neither did Jesus.

Believing in Jesus is fine, but it makes no sense to "believe" in him and not do what he said, which is to love God and love one another. The Bible says even demons believe in Jesus.[6] They know beyond a shadow of a doubt that he is the Son of God, one with the Father. But it doesn't do them any good, because they are absolutely against love.

Jesus actually warned against thinking that belief alone would save us. One time Jesus told his disciples, "Not everyone who says to me, 'Lord! Lord!' will enter the kingdom of heaven, but only the person who does the will of my Father who is in heaven."[7]

Again, in another place, Jesus describes the final judgment. Those who enter heaven are those who gave food and drink to the hungry and thirsty, clothing to the naked, shelter to the homeless, and friendship to the sick and imprisoned. Those who enter hell refused to do all these things.[8] What's the principle here? Love of neighbor. Those who enter heaven have it; those who enter hell don't.

So Why Bother with Jesus?

You might ask, "If the final judgment is just going to be about how we have loved, why bother believing in Jesus at all? Why don't I just go and love people, and it will all be good, with or without Jesus?"

That's an absolutely great question, and I'm glad you asked it.

First, the Bible does say it's possible for those who didn't know of Jesus to enter heaven because they did what was right. Paul the missionary summed up the final judgment like this: "God will give to every man according to his works: to those who seek for glory and honor and immortality by patiently doing what is good, he will give eternal life; but for those who like to argue and do not follow the truth, but follow wickedness, there will be wrath and fury."[9]

So why not strike out on our own, without the help of Jesus?

To me, this is kind of like saying, "Why don't I just swim the Atlantic rather than taking a boat?"

There are at least four reasons why I would never "strike out on my own" to try to enter heaven:

1. Forgiveness. I mess up every day. I know very well what is good and what is bad, what is loving and what is not, according to Jesus' teaching. I've been reading the life of Jesus and the teachings of the apostles every day since I was a boy. Still, not a day goes by when I don't realize, at some point, that I've done something unloving. Sometimes it's in small things, and sometimes it's in a big way.

I need forgiveness for this. Why do I turn my back on God in so many little (or big) ways? I don't always know, but I *do* know I need the forgiveness that Jesus offers. Jesus' best student, John, once said: "If we confess our sins, he is faithful and just, and will forgive our sins and wash us from all injustice."[10]

A gift is free
but must be accepted

Jesus can forgive in God's name because he is God and because he has suffered for all the evil we have done. I need that forgiveness on a daily basis. I would never want to be without it. I would want you and everyone to have this forgiveness too. It is free, but you have to choose to accept it.

2. Help. I need strength to do better. Living a life of love is hard. If people think it's easy, it's because they haven't tried it, or else they don't understand what love involves.

Jesus says that to be perfect, we need to love even our enemies. That's hard for me to do. That's more love than I can muster from inside myself. But Jesus promises to share with us God's own love so that we can go beyond ourselves. Paul the great missionary put it like this: "God's love has been poured into our hearts through the Holy Spirit who has been given to us."[11]

I know that Jesus has put his love inside of me, through my baptism. I don't always let his love work through me. But when I do, I am able to love in ways beyond my own strength.

3. Guidance. I need Jesus' teachings to help me see right from wrong, to see what is loving in each situation.

Love is not the same thing as niceness. Sometimes love means confronting people with how they are hurting others and themselves.

In ancient Rome, gladiator contests were very popular. People enjoyed going to the stadium to watch men kill each other in combat. That's pretty sick. However, people were so used to it, and liked it so much, that they didn't see it as wrong. Followers of Jesus spoke out against these contests, but people didn't listen. They just got angry.

These death contests didn't end until at least one Christian got killed walking out into the stadium trying to stop them. Finally, this woke up the consciences of enough people that the government put an end to the practice.

There are many things like that. In every culture, we mistreat others in ways we don't recognize. We do it in private and in public. We can be blinded by our own culture and not see right from wrong. Without the guidance of Jesus, we may spend our lives doing what our culture says is right, only to find out at the final judgment that it was all wrong.

I need Jesus' guidance. His teaching helps me to see right from wrong, love from unlove, from God's perspective and not just by American standards, which are often pretty lame.

4. Love of God. Finally, I need Jesus because he is God, and God is love. Although loving other people is important, we can't forget that God is a person too. In fact, he is the first person in our lives, the person who is always with us—from our mother's womb till we are placed in the tomb, and also in the life to come.

God deserves to be loved, because he loves us and gave us everything we are and have.

Jesus taught us to love others but to love God first. Why? Is that prideful of God? Is God selfish? Does he want us to love him more than other people because he is jealous?

No. God is love. He is the source of all love. When I love God first, I get filled with his love and can love others *better*.

Trying to love others by myself is like a fire engine that pumps water on the blaze from its own tanks. When I love God first, it's like connecting to the hydrant. Now I don't need to worry about my tanks running out. I have a limitless supply of love to share with others.

If it's true that Jesus is God, it would just be odd to ignore him and try to get to heaven without him.

1. The Gospel of Matthew 12:30.

2. The First Letter of St. John 4:8, 16.

3. See, for example, the Gospel of Matthew 8:12; 22:13; the Book of Revelation 19 and 20.

4. See the Gospel of Matthew 25:41.

5. See C.S. Lewis, *The Problem of Pain* (New York: HarperCollins, 1996), 131.

6. See the Epistle of James 2:19: "You believe that God is one; you do well. Even the demons believe—and shudder."

7. See the Gospel of Matthew 7:21.

8. See the Gospel of Matthew 25:31-46.

9. See the Epistle of St. Paul to the Romans 2:6-9.

10. See the First Letter of St. John 1:9.

11. The Epistle of St. Paul to the Romans 5:5.

Chapter 9

What If I Say Yes to Jesus?

You might wonder: if I say yes to Jesus, what's the fine print? What do I have to do? Pray a prayer? Light a candle? Wear a tee-shirt or a wristband for the rest of my life?

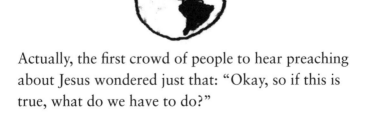

Actually, the first crowd of people to hear preaching about Jesus wondered just that: "Okay, so if this is true, what do we have to do?"

The answer has not changed in two thousand years.

The book of the Bible we call the Acts of the Apostles records a time when Peter preached about Jesus to a great crowd of people in Jerusalem.[1] Several thousand listeners were deeply moved. The Bible says, "They were cut to the heart, and said to Peter and the rest of the apostles, 'Brothers, what shall we do?'"

And Peter said to them, "Repent, and be baptized every one of you in the name of Jesus Christ for the forgiveness of your sins, and you will receive the gift of the Holy Spirit."

A lot of people followed Peter's advice. The Bible records this: "So those who received his word were baptized, and about three thousand people were added that day."

Added to what? Added to the early Church.

And what did these newly baptized disciples of Jesus do? The Bible says, "They devoted themselves
to the apostles' teaching
and fellowship,
to the breaking of bread
and the prayers."

That's it in a nutshell. Those are *still* the steps we have to take if we believe in Jesus.

Let's break it down into single steps and explain each one.

1. Repent!

The first thing Peter said is that we have to repent. This means "to turn around," quit the bad stuff we've been doing, and start over with a new life.

Repenting involves both feelings and actions. It involves feeling sadness for the bad that we have done in our lives: all the selfish and unloving behavior, all the ways we've lied, cheated, or manipulated to get what we want.

It also involves taking action: we can't keep on living the same way. We have to take steps to live a different life. The way we talk, the way we act, and especially

Yes, There Is a God

the way we treat people must change. It's going to
be a process, but it's a process we have to commit
to, today. God will help us carry it out. It won't be
something we have to do on our own. More on that
below.

2. Be Baptized!

After repenting, Peter tells us we need to "be baptized,
every one of you, in the name of Jesus Christ for the
forgiveness of your sins."

What is baptism? Baptism is a ceremony of washing,
where water is poured over the body. It means many
things, including the washing away of sin. Jesus
promised that those who were washed in his name
would receive God's Spirit, the Holy Spirit, into their
hearts.

Baptism also means a new birth, a new start in life. In
ancient times, it was not just followers of Jesus who

were baptized. Other groups used baptism as a sign that someone was starting a new life as a follower of a certain teaching.

If you believe Jesus is who he claimed to be, you have to get baptized.

Baptism is a public statement that you've begun a new life following Jesus. It's a bright line between your old life and your new life. It tells the world you've decided to follow Jesus and there's no turning back.

Peter says baptism is "for the forgiveness of sins." Through baptism, Jesus forgives all our sins.

One time Jesus was having a conversation with a Jewish leader named Nicodemus. He wanted to understand Jesus' teaching about God. Jesus explained, "Unless one is born of water and the Spirit, he cannot enter the kingdom of God."

Nicodemus didn't understand what Jesus was talking about. "How can a man enter a second time into his mother's womb to be born?" he asked.

But Jesus was talking about baptism. Baptism is a spiritual birth by water and God's spirit. Jesus gives us forgiveness of sins and God's Spirit when we are baptized.[2]

3. Receive the Holy Spirit!

Jesus promised that those who were baptized would receive God's own Spirit, which we call the Holy Spirit.

The Holy Spirit makes us children of God. If having the same DNA is what makes us family with our parents, then having the same Spirit is what makes us family with God. This all goes back to Jesus' teaching that God is our Father.

The gift of the Holy Spirit is usually not something you can feel. Some people do have strong sensations when they are baptized; they "feel" something different. But most do not have any physical sensation.

That's because our five senses are not designed to sense God. They sense flavor, sound, light, textures, and odors, but not "God-ness." God is not a physical being. Since we don't have a sixth sense that can feel God, we can't rely on "feeling" if God is around or in us. We have to trust Jesus' promise that the Spirit is given through baptism.

The Holy Spirit in your life will help you to see what is good and evil and to want the good even when it means suffering.

The Holy Spirit will help you live a new life, by giving you the desire to grow closer to God. Many young Christians have a spiritual "high" after baptism or confirmation, when their desire to be close to God is very strong for some time. This can be the work of the Holy Spirit. But those desires have to be channeled. If those desires don't lead us to taking practical steps to lead a new life, they can fade away without changing us.

So that's where these next steps come in. We need to imitate those first Christians, who "devoted themselves to the apostles' teaching and fellowship,

to the breaking of bread and the prayers." There are four things here that are basic to being and staying a disciple of Jesus:
the apostles' teaching,
fellowship,
breaking of bread,
and prayer.

4. Devote Yourself to the Apostles' Teaching!

We need to remember that being a disciple means being a student. And a student studies. Jesus taught us a lot. Jesus' best student, John, said, "If everything Jesus said and did were written down, I suppose all the world could not hold the books that would be written."[3] You can spend your whole life studying Jesus' teachings and still not get bored.

Jesus never wrote anything down. He only taught by word of mouth. That is why we rely on the *apostles' teaching* in order to know about him and his message.

All of the apostles taught about Jesus by word of mouth, and some of them wrote the message down or had others write it down. That's how we got our four biographies, or "Gospels," by Matthew, Mark, Luke, and John.

The apostles also taught on a number of issues that came up after Jesus ascended to heaven. These teachings are contained mostly in their letters. Most of the books in the New Testament part of the Bible are letters from the apostles to different local churches. These letters are an important record of the apostles' teaching.

At its heart, much of Jesus' teaching is very simple: for example, love God, and love your neighbor. But life is not simple. In practice, it's not always easy to know how to love.

For example, your friend may ask you to buy him a beer. Giving people what they ask for can often be a sign of love. But is it if your friend is an alcoholic? In such a situation, it is not loving to buy him a beer. It might put him back on the road of addiction. Love in this case may mean saying no, and your friend may not appreciate it. So loving someone in this case may mean telling him no and making him mad.

And that is a pretty simple example. There are much more complicated situations. For that reason, we need help in learning what true love is. Our own gut instincts are not always right. Neither are the opinions of our friends, TV celebrities, or politicians.

We have a tendency to see the world through our own glasses. "Love" often seems to be whatever feels good for us at the moment.

Jesus and his apostles shed a lot of light on what is good and what is evil, what is love and what is not. Their teaching helps us to learn to recognize when we are fooling ourselves and manipulating a situation. Their teaching helps us to recognize what is truly loving, even if it means saying no.

Learning is a lifelong process. In practice, being devoted to the apostles' teaching means reading and mentally "chewing" on the books of the New Testament, or listening to them read and explained at church, on a weekly or daily basis.

It's a good idea to get yourself your own Bible. Make sure the English translation is readable for you. Then, read for a few minutes each day from the Gospels: Matthew, Mark, Luke, John. The Holy Spirit will help you learn as you read. In fact, it's as if the Holy Spirit speaks to you through the words on the page. Our relationship with God is like a conversation: when we pray, we speak to God. And when we read the Gospels, God speaks to us. The Gospels are like letters from a loving father.

When you become very familiar with the Gospels, you can branch out into other parts of the Bible. A good friend or your pastor can guide you and suggest other books that can help you understand the Bible better.

5. Devote Yourself to Fellowship!

Fellowship means friendship, or "hanging out" with others: talking with them and sharing our lives with them.

family of God

Jesus wasn't a loner and didn't teach people to be loners. He taught large groups of people, and he always had friends around. He spoke of the "family of God" and called people his "brothers and sisters" when they tried to do God's will.

Jesus also spoke of building the "kingdom of God," which was a community of people who follow God. This community is called "the Church."

No one should be a "Lone Ranger Christian." The Christian lifestyle means being part of a family, the Church. The Church ("big C") is a worldwide reality of all followers of Jesus. But it is also a local reality, with several local churches ("small c")—one of which is probably within easy driving distance of you and me.

Songwriter Bill Withers used to sing, "We all need somebody to lean on." That's true when you are trying to follow Jesus. Jesus said, "The way that leads to destruction is wide and smooth. The way that leads to life is difficult and narrow."[4] And people on a difficult journey bring friends for support. Hikers on Mount Everest travel in groups. They know that some things are too hard to be done alone.

In practice, if you are serious about following Jesus, you are going to need good friendships with people who are doing the same thing. And you are not going to meet those people unless you commit to a local church and spend time there—worshipping, praying, and hanging out with other disciples. We'll talk more about which church to join later.

7. Devote Yourself to the "Breaking of Bread"!

The "breaking of bread" is the early name for a common meal of bread and wine that Jesus taught his followers to share. This meal is now usually called "the Eucharist" (YOU-car-ist) or just "the Mass." I can't stress enough how important this meal was to Jesus and his followers.

Jesus taught his followers, "Unless you eat my flesh and drink my blood, you have no life in you. He who eats my flesh and drinks my blood has eternal life, and I will raise him up at the last day."[5]

This sounded pretty gross, so many of Jesus' followers left him when he taught this. They could not figure out what he meant.

On the night before his death, Jesus shared a Jewish Passover meal with his disciples. When he passed out the bread for the meal, he said, "Take, eat; this is my body."[6]

He also took a cup of wine and said, "Drink of it, all of you; for this is my blood of the covenant."[7] A covenant is a family bond. Jesus was making a family bond between God and human beings.

Since the first Easter Sunday when Jesus rose from the dead, his followers have been gathering on the first day of the week to share a common meal of bread and wine, repeating Jesus' words, "This is my body; this is my blood."

In two thousand years, not a single Sunday has passed when there weren't Christians somewhere, gathering for the "breaking of the bread." To this day, hundreds of millions gather around the world, on every continent, every week.

How is it his body and blood? That is difficult to understand.

That it is his body and blood? This is something Jesus' followers take as true, just because he said it was.

It's not magic, but one might call it a miracle. Jesus promised that he would always be present to his followers, until the end of time. And one of the ways he is present is through his wine-blood and bread-body of this meal.

If we believe Jesus' words, "Unless you eat my flesh and drink my blood, you have no life in you,"[8] then we have to find a local church that serves his body and blood every week. And there are such churches that have kept this custom for thousands of years. They are usually called "Catholic." We'll talk more about how to choose a local church later.

8. Devote Yourself to Prayer!

Prayer is talking to God. It can take many forms. There are memorized prayers that we can recite, and there is free prayer, in which we just talk to God about whatever is on our mind.

Jesus did both, and so have Christians ever since.

There are four basic things we usually do in prayer:

The first is to worship God, to praise him for who he is.
The second is to confess our sins, our failings.
The third is to thank him for all the good things in our life.
The fourth is to ask for the things we need for ourselves and others.

Jesus himself prayed, sometimes spending the whole night in prayer.

If Jesus himself needed it, we sure do.

For Jesus, prayer was a conversation with his Father. It can be similar for us. We have already talked about how God speaks to us through the Bible, and how we answer back through prayer. But sometimes God even "talks" to us in prayer as well.

It's very rare for a person to hear the voice of God audibly in prayer, although it has happened. Perhaps it's good that it doesn't usually happen, because it would probably be frightening. Instead, God usually works in a quieter way.

Sometimes in prayer, God will put a thought in our heart that we know wasn't there before.

Sometimes in prayer, we begin to see clearly what God wants us to do in a certain situation.

In these quiet ways, God guides us in prayer. As with any relationship, over time we get to know the person better. Over time, through prayer, we come to know God better. We become more aware of when he is guiding us.

It's usually recommended that we start off by setting aside fifteen minutes for prayer each day. As your relationship with God grows, you will probably want to increase your prayer time.

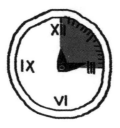

Besides personal prayer, there is also group prayer.

It's very important for the followers of Jesus to gather together for prayer. The most important time this happens is on Sunday, the day Jesus rose from the dead, when we gather to break bread. We always pray a lot when we gather to break bread. Sometimes it's hard to stay focused, because the prayers are mostly the same, but it's important to be present and try our best to pray along with everyone else. The followers of Jesus are family, after all.

So That's All We Have to Do?

Is that all we have to do if we believe in Jesus?

In a nutshell, yes. As Peter said, "Repent, be baptized, and receive the Holy Spirit." Then, devote yourself to the apostles' teaching, fellowship, the breaking of bread, and prayer.

It's simple, but it's a lot. It's a big change of life, but on the other hand, we are not doing this on our own. God promises the gift of his Spirit. St. Paul once said, "It is no longer I who live, but Christ who lives in me."[9] What we are doing is inviting God into our lives, to take over.

If you choose to follow this way of life, you are going to learn a lot when you start devoting yourself to the apostles' teaching, for example. If you are like me, you'll find out that there are many unloving habits you haven't noticed before in your life. Things will have to change. But Jesus is with us to help us change, if we let him.

One of the ways Jesus helps us is through his other followers, who may be a little further down the road than we are. Keep in mind that the followers of Jesus have been around for a long time and know what we need for this journey. So they have built "rest areas"—or churches—for those traveling down this road.

When you buy your first car and it runs out of gas for the first time, you know you need to fill it up. And guess what? You're not the first to think of that problem. People have built gas stations all over the place to make sure you can do just that.

It's similar in the life of following Jesus. When we decide to follow him and need a place to break bread and pray, suddenly we discover that there already are churches all over the place to meet that need. You'll need to choose one and become part of it. Which one to choose? We'll talk about that in another chapter.

1. See the Acts of the Apostles 2:14-42.

2. See the Gospel of John 3:1-21.

3. See the Gospel of John 21:25.

4. See the Gospel of Matthew 7:13-14.

5. See the Gospel of John 6:53-54.

6. The Gospel of Matthew 26:26.

7. The Gospel of Matthew 26:27-28.

8. See the Gospel of John 6:53.

9. The Epistle of St. Paul to the Galatians 2:20.

Chapter 10

Which Church Did Jesus Start?

"Okay, so I need to find a local church to join if I want to follow Jesus. Which one should I choose?"

This can be hard because there are so many different Christian groups. You may have heard of some of them: Baptist, Lutheran, Reformed, Pentecostal, Charismatic, Presbyterian, Orthodox, and many others. The technical term for these different groups is "denominations."

There are many wonderful things about all of these groups. Most of them have many important things in common, especially a love for Jesus and a desire to follow him faithfully.

However, I must be honest and say that there are important differences between them too. I personally spent much of my life trying to figure out which one to belong to. And so, with love to everyone, I want to share with you some of the reasons that led me to the church I call my home.

One church really stands out from all the rest for a number of reasons: its size, its age, its unity, and its diversity. It's the largest, oldest, and most diverse of any one church. That's the church called "Catholic."

"Catholic"

Catholic is a very old Greek word. It comes from the time when Jesus lived, when Greek was the world language, as English is today. *Catholic* in Greek means "international" or "universal."

After the twelve apostles passed on, the main group
of Jesus' followers began to call themselves the
"Catholic" Church. Later, other groups broke off
from the Catholic Church because they disagreed with
some of its teachings. But only the Catholic Church
can say that its teachings were handed down from the
apostles themselves through an unbroken chain of
bishops to today.

As I said, the name "Catholic" means "universal,"
and the name stuck to this day.

Size

The Catholic Church is impressive in size. About half
of all Christians, or about one billion people in the
world, identify with this Church. It's about the size
of all other Christian groups combined. Being big
doesn't make the Catholic Church correct. But there is
clearly something about the Catholic Church that has
worked for *a lot* of people.

Age

The Catholic Church is impressive in age. It's the oldest human organization still in existence. Its leaders go back to Jesus' own apostles.

Consider this: everyone the world over knows that the leader of the Catholic Church is a man named Francis. His title is "pope," a very old word that just means "father." Before Francis, the pope was a man named Benedict. And before him, a man named John Paul II. Now, how far back can we keep this up?

It turns out, pretty far. The line of popes goes all the way back before the 100s. In AD 99, the pope was a man named Clement. He followed a man named Anacletus, who followed Linus, who followed Peter, Jesus' right-hand man and the first leader of the "catholic" or universal church.

In this way, the Catholic Church can prove its existence back to the time of Jesus. In fact, you could almost say the Catholic Church is literally built on the apostles.

For example, when the pope leads worship in St. Peter's Basilica in Rome, he is standing almost right over the tomb of St. Peter himself. Many of Peter's bones are still in that tomb.

You might say, how do we know it is the tomb of Peter?

Archeologists have gone down and examined it. They found an ancient inscription on it that says, "Here is Peter." Inside the tomb are many bones of a man dated to the time of Jesus. The archeologists also found evidence that people had been praying at this tomb for a long time—basically, from around the time Peter died.

According to historical records, people knew it was the tomb of Peter, and that's why they built a church over it. There has been a church on the site since the 300s. That's over seventeen hundred years!

That's about as much historical proof as we can reasonably ask for. After all, we can't expect to find Peter's driver's license and passport in the tomb.

Diversity

These days there is a lot of talk about diversity. In a sense, the Catholic Church is a church for modern times: it's the most diverse human organization that's still *one* organization.

As we said before, the word *Catholic* means "international" or "universal," and you will not find a group that better lives up to the name. There are Catholics from every country of the world. I live in America, but I bump into Catholics from Africa, China, Vietnam, France, Germany, Italy, England, Mexico, all the countries of South America, India, the Philippines, Taiwan, and many other places. The Catholic Church has spread all over. It has deep roots in many cultures and many nations. It's not tied to one culture or one country.

Yet for all that, the teaching is the same wherever you go. The language, clothing, and music may be very different, but the teaching is the same. To me, that's remarkable.

Yet it makes sense. If God has spoken to humanity, you'd think he'd speak the same message to everyone.

Jesus clearly claimed to be God and to speak to all humanity. The disciple John summed it up when he said, "God so loved the world that he sent his one and only Son, that whoever trusts in him would not perish, but would have eternal life."[1]

Jesus came for the world. So we should look for a church that is as big as the world and is open to the world. The Catholic Church is that. It is big, it is ancient, and it is universal. That's why I recommend it to you.

The Catholic Church still carries the torch for Jesus. It holds on to his original teaching and remembers what he said. I found this out for myself later in life. When I was about thirty, I read for the first time the writings of the early Christian pastors, the ones who knew the apostles and carried on after their deaths. I discovered that they taught all the same basics that the Catholic Church still teaches today. These early Christians were Catholic and even called themselves that. I was impressed. I figured, if it was good enough for the first

Christians, it's good enough for me. So I became a Catholic.

The Catholic Church is very ancient and even *looks* ancient. When you visit a Catholic church for worship, you're going to see men dressed in robes like those worn in the time of Jesus.

You may see young men carrying candles, because in the time of Jesus, there was no electricity.

Some parts of the service may be in ancient languages spoken in the time of Jesus.

Catholic worship has a different feel than what's on TV or in the local mall. That's because the Catholic Church is trying to stay faithful to what Jesus taught us, even to the point of keeping some of the ancient ways.

If you choose to believe in Jesus, I recommend you call a local Catholic church. Ask to talk to the pastor. He may be out and have to call you back. No matter. When you talk to him, tell him you're interested in becoming a Christian. He should be happy and helpful and tell you what you need to do.

If he's not, call a different Catholic church, until you find a pastor who is happy to talk to you. Sadly, some pastors get tired out with all the work they have to do. But you're going to need someone who's not too tired to help you with your new life with God. I'm sure you'll find a pastor like that near you.

1. See the Gospel of John 3:16.

Chapter 11
Four Possibilities

Now that we've explored the teaching and person of Jesus, we have to make a decision about him.

We've seen that there's pretty strong scientific evidence for God, or at least for an intelligent creator, which is what we mean by the word "God." The evidence is so strong that even some atheist scientists have admitted it makes them uncomfortable.

We've seen that a lot of people are convinced that Jesus spoke to us from God. There is so much more testimony about him than any other person in human history. Christians believe he speaks for God. The Quran says he speaks for God. Even many Jewish leaders have been impressed with him.

We've seen that Jesus called us to repent and to love God and others. He suffered and died for us, to absorb all the punishment our selfishness deserves. He offers forgiveness, strength, and eternal life to anyone who will accept it from him.

If we want to accept Jesus, we need to repent and be baptized to receive God's Spirit. Then we need to commit ourselves to a new life of being Jesus' students or "disciples."

Now we have to make a decision about what to do. I guess there are four possibilities in front of us:

(1) We can say, "This all sounds nice, but it's not true," and in the end, it turns out not to be true. Jesus really isn't God, etc. Something else turns out to be true. That would be an okay outcome.

(2) We can say, "It's not true," but it turns out to be true. That would be kind of awkward in the afterlife, as we try to explain to Jesus why we rejected him, even though his plan was explained to us. That would not be a good outcome. It could end with our being cut off from God permanently.

(3) We can say, "It's true; I trust Jesus!" but it turns out to be false in the end. How bad would that be? We would spend our lives chasing a beautiful ideal of self-giving love by making acts of sacrifice to love others. It turns out to be false in the end. So we missed out on what everyone else was doing: trying to get as much profit, pleasure, and power as they legally could before they died.

For myself, I'm not sure this is a bad outcome. Even if the Jesus story is false, I'd rather chase his vision than follow the other lifestyles out there. Every week the supermarket tabloids are full of stories about people who chased it all, got it all, and end up miserable. I think love, self-sacrifice, and faithfulness make for a better life even here and now.

(4) We can say, "It's all true, and I believe!" and it turns out to be true. In that case, we really win the jackpot. In this life, we discover peace and new meaning. We get God's love and strength to overcome hardship. And in the next life, we experience peace and joy with God the Father, Son, and Spirit and all holy people forever and ever. Everything is Love in the end. That's a pretty good outcome. I'm willing to take a risk to gain that.

So what decision should you make?

The way I see it, the only really long-term bad outcome would be to reject Jesus by mistake. Following him may mean short-term sacrifices, but in the long term, it seems like a safe option.

In the end, though, I didn't make my own decision about Jesus based on odds, like a gambling man.

I made my decision out of love. I fell in love with Jesus. Although I respect other great world teachers and leaders, none of them speak to me of self-giving love the way Jesus does. He touches a chord deep inside of me. In fact, I've come to believe he loved me long before I loved him. Through the Holy Spirit, he's living in me now.

You will make your own decision. If you want to follow Jesus, I'd encourage you to call a local Catholic Church and ask for baptism.

Or maybe you're just not sure yet. I get that. It takes a while for things to gel. You might want to check out other options to make sure they aren't right.

My gut tells me that if you really want truth, your path will take you back to Jesus in the end. When it does, the followers of Jesus in the Catholic Church will be here, waiting to help you!

Appendix

In Chapter 2, I present some arguments for the existence of God. For those who are interested, here are some further resources.

(1) Looking Up: The Cosmological Argument for God

In the section in Chapter 2 called "Looking Up," I present one of the strongest and most basic reasons to believe in God's existence. Philosophers call it the "Cosmological Argument," and perhaps its simplest form is the "Kalam," which goes like this:

Point 1: Anything that begins to exist has a cause.
Point 2: The universe began to exist.
Point 3: Therefore, the universe has a cause.

A very helpful presentation of this argument is here: http://www.reasonablefaith.org/kalam.

No one can reasonably doubt Point 1, because if things can begin to exist with no cause, we have to admit that the universe is irrational, and anything can happen for no reason at all. We should have no objection to elephants appearing in the dining room, because we have granted the principle that things can happen with no cause.

No one can reasonably doubt Point 2 either, because we know the universe is winding down and running out of usable energy. Therefore, it cannot be infinitely old, or else it would have already run out of energy. So the universe did have a beginning; scientists place the Big Bang as happening about 14.5 billion years ago. Yet we need to remember what Einstein's theories show: the Big Bang was not only the beginning of matter and energy, but also of *space* and *time*.

Therefore, the *cause* of the Big Bang must itself be outside space and time. And it must be powerful and intelligent, because the universe is extremely big and bears the mark of astounding intelligent arrangement.

(2) Looking Down: An Argument from the Complexity of Life

In this section, I argue that even the simplest biological life is too complex to have developed just by chance and natural processes.

To get an idea of how complex life is, it is helpful to watch online the animations of the chemical processes at work inside a cell:

The Inner Life of the Cell (XVIVO Scientific Animations): https://www.youtube.com/watch?v=wJyUtbn0O5Y.

Drew Berry, "Animations of Unseeable Biology," from TEDxSydney 2011: https://www.youtube.com/watch?v=WFCvkkDSfIU.

I highly recommend this entire video on the subject of the origin of life, *Unlocking the Mystery of Life*, from Illustra Media, available here: http://go2rpi.com/unlocking-the-mystery-of-life-dvd/. *Unlocking the Mystery of Life* is also available for instant streaming on Amazon.com, and in various formats on YouTube.

Claiming that life could not arise by chance is controversial, because of the popularity of Darwin's theory of evolution in the culture and in schools.

However, Darwin never gave an explanation for the origin of life itself, just the development of life forms once it had begun. To this day, no scientist has been able to provide a working model of how life could come from non-life. This is not my own idea. If you don't believe me, read the article by science journalist John Horgan called "Pssst! Don't tell the creationists, but scientists don't have a clue how life began" on the blog of the prestigious journal *Scientific American* (Feb. 28, 2011).[1] Or read the quotes from researchers listed below.[2]

But what *did* Darwin teach? Darwin thought single-celled life forms were similar to animated lumps of clear gelatin, because that is what they looked like under his primitive microscopes.

So in a February 1, 1871 letter to his friend Joseph Dalton Hooker, he wrote that perhaps life had begun when a spark of electricity (presumably lightning) occurred in a "warm little pond" of nutrient-rich water on the early earth.[3]

We now know, of course, that nothing like this can work. Electrical sparks in a nutrient-rich solution will never produce anything more than amino acids, the building blocks of the proteins necessary for life; but the proteins themselves are far beyond the reach of such simple processes.[4] Moreover, DNA and RNA will not naturally form in water, because its bonds are established through dehydration synthesis (a drying process).[5]

Yet even the theoretically simplest form of life imaginable would need at least 250 different proteins to survive and at least RNA to reproduce.[6]

That's why Dr. Harold P. Klein of Santa Clara University, the chairman of a National Academy of Sciences committee that reviewed research on the origin of life, was quoted as saying, "The simplest bacterium is so damn complicated from the point of view of a chemist that it is almost impossible to imagine how it happened."[7]

For more quotes from scientists on the complexity of life, see here: http://theoutlet.us/Quotesoncomplexityofcellandoriginoflife.pdf.

(3) Looking Around

Here is a website that gives excellent basic information about cosmic fine-tuning: http://www.godandscience.org/apologetics/designun.html.

My favorite resource on cosmic fine-tuning is the film *The Privileged Planet*, available here: http://go2rpi.com/privileged-planet-dvd/.

You can also search for *Privileged Planet* on Amazon for instant streaming (just $2) or on YouTube. The film is based on a book by Jay Richards and Guillermo Gonzales, *The Privileged Planet* (Washington, DC: Regnery, 2004).

If you have a very strong science and philosophy background, you can tackle the book by Fr. Robert Spitzer, *New Proofs for the Existence of God* (Grand Rapids: Eerdmans, 2010), which gives one of the most technical discussions of fine-tuning and its implications available in print.

When I have shared about cosmic fine-tuning and the anthropic principle with atheists, some have responded that fine-tuning is just in the imagination of creationists or religious believers. However, that is clearly not true. Many atheists have admitted that fine-tuning is a problem for atheism.

The famous atheist physicist Stephen Hawking, in his book *A Brief History of Time*, admitted that fine-tuning was "remarkable" and could be understood as evidence for God.[8]

The atheist Sir Fred Hoyle, a British physicist and astronomer knighted for his scholarly achievements, famously said about fine-tuning: "A common sense interpretation of the facts suggests that a super intellect has 'monkeyed' with the physics as well as the chemistry and biology, and there are no blind forces worth speaking about in nature."[9]

Discover magazine ran a story in December 2008 entitled, "Science's Alternative to an Intelligent Creator: The Multiverse Theory."[10] The article frankly admitted that cosmic fine-tuning was such strong evidence for a creator that atheist scientists were working on a theory of an infinite number of universes, so that our specially designed one would not be surprising. With an infinite number of universes, at least one would be sure to have amazing fine-tuning necessary for life, right? The only problem is that there is currently no observational evidence of any universe other than our own. So, this is literally a case of persons being willing to believe in *anything* and *everything* rather than a God.

(4) Looking Inside: The Moral Argument

On the moral argument, here are a few further resources:

http://www.reasonablefaith.org/moral
http://www.reasonablefaith.org/media/moral-argument-video.

1. This is the URL: https://blogs.scientificamerican.com/cross-check/pssst-dont-tell-the-creationists-but-scientists-dont-have-a-clue-how-life-began/.

2. See http://theoutlet.us/Quotesoncomplexityofcellandoriginoflife.pdf.

3. For the text of Darwin's letter, search for "Hooker 1 February 1871" at www.darwinproject.ac.uk.

4. Sir Fred Hoyle, "The Universe: Past and Present Reflections," in *Engineering and Science* (November 1981), pp. 8–12.

5. On dehydration synthesis, see: https://www.youtube.com/watch?v=Udq7dX7jJMw .

6. See W. Wells, "Taking Life to Bits," in *New Scientist* 155 (1997), pp. 30-33.

7. John Horgan, "In the Beginning," *Scientific American* (February 1991), p. 120.

8. Stephen Hawking, *A Brief History of Time* (New York: Bantam, 1988), p. 127, speaking of the fine-tuning involved in most Big Bang models: "It would be very difficult to explain why the universe should have begun in just this way, except as the act of a God who intended to create beings like us." To be clear, Hawking holds to a controversial alternate model of the origins involving something called "imaginary time" that enables him to believe the universe is eternal and thus does not need a creator. Few scientists or philosophers have adopted Hawking's model.

9. Fred Hoyle, *Annual Review of Astronomy and Astrophysics* 20 (1982), p. 16.

10. http://discovermagazine.com/2008/dec/10-sciences-alternative-to-an-intelligent-creator.

the WORD
among us ®
The *Spirit* of Catholic Living

This book was published by The Word Among Us. Since 1981, The Word Among Us has been answering the call of the Second Vatican Council to help Catholic laypeople encounter Christ in the Scriptures.

The name of our company comes from the prologue to the Gospel of John and reflects the vision and purpose of all of our publications: to be an instrument of the Spirit, whose desire is to manifest Jesus' presence in and to the children of God. In this way, we hope to contribute to the Church's ongoing mission of proclaiming the gospel to the world so that all people would know the love and mercy of our Lord and grow more deeply in their faith as missionary disciples.

Our monthly devotional magazine, *The Word Among Us*, features meditations on the daily and Sunday Mass readings, and currently reaches more than one million Catholics in North America and another half million Catholics in one hundred countries around the world. Our book division, The Word Among Us Press, publishes numerous books, Bible studies, and pamphlets that help Catholics grow in their faith.

To learn more about who we are and what we publish, log on to our website at www.wau.org. There you will find a variety of Catholic resources that will help you grow in your faith.

Embrace His Word, Listen to God . . .

www.wau.org